W9-BVG-603

LIVING
WITH ROYALTY

CLOVIS
CHAPPELL

Living with Royalty

ABINGDON PRESS
new york • nashville

LIVING WITH ROYALTY

Library of Congress Catalog Card Number: 62-11520

SET UP, PRINTED, AND BOUND BY THE PARTHENON PRESS, AT NASHVILLE, TENNESSEE, UNITED STATES OF AMERICA

CONTENTS

I. THE ACID TEST (INTRODUCTORY)

He did what was right in the eyes of the Lord.
—II KINGS 18:3
He did what was evil in the sight of the Lord.
—II KINGS 21:2

In the following pages we are to live a few brief hours with royalty. The inspired writers who tell us of these ancient kings are interested in all that was meaningful to the kings. They are concerned with their parentage, with their marriages and their children. They are concerned with their wars, with their defeats and victories. They are interested in the love and loyalty they won from their subjects—and also in the antagonism and hatred they aroused. They tell us how some died in honor, their graves decorated by a nation's praise. They tell us how others died in dishonor, how one was even given the burial of an ass.

But while they are interested in all the interests of these kings, their victories and defeats, their glory and their shame—these are all secondary. Their one supreme interest is this: How did they stand with reference to the will of

God? These words, "He did what was evil in the sight of the Lord" or "He did what was right in the eyes of the Lord," run through every story like a refrain. All else they did, all else they failed to do, was of secondary importance. The one thing that matters supremely is this: Did they live within the will of God, or did they rebel against that will?

Why do these inspired writers take this narrow view? They do so because they were wise enough to know that nothing else eternally matters. Triumphs and tragedies are temporary and passing, but "He who does the will of God abides for ever." There is absolutely nothing that can enable us to live victoriously if we flout the will of God. It is equally true that nothing can defeat us if we live within the will of God. Here, then, is the one matter which counts supremely, whatever our position, whatever our century.

I

The first fact that these texts bring before us is that God had a will for these men of high position and responsibility. He had a definite plan for each one of these kings. It was his will that they should live and act according to that plan. He knew that they would bring help or hurt to themselves and to their subjects only in proportion to the fullness with which they entered into that plan. I think it is fairly easy for us to believe this.

What is a bit harder to believe, however, is that God no more planned the lives of these ancient kings than he plans your life and mine. This should be credible in light of the fact that ours is a rational universe, a planned world. If such were not the case, no science would be possible. What could the ablest scientist learn in a world of chance? What could he learn in a world where gravity acted one moment and failed to act the next, or where the same fire would sometimes boil water and sometimes freeze it? Nothing in our world walks with aimless feet. The very stars speak of a planning God.

> In reason's ear they all rejoice,
> And utter forth a glorious voice;
> For ever singing as they shine,
> "The Hand that made us is divine."
>
> —JOSEPH ADDISON, *Ode*

Surely, if God plans the visible things that are to last but for a day, he will also plan your life and mine who are to last through eternity. This conviction runs throughout the Bible. For instance, Jeremiah went one day to visit a certain potter. When he entered this ancient manufacturing establishment, three objects at once caught and held his attention. First, there was a man at work—the potter. Second, there was that with which he worked—a wheel. Third, there was that upon he worked—a bit of plastic clay which he was seeking to shape into a vase or cup.

I can imagine that the prophet, being curious, touched this potter on the shoulder and asked, "Just what kind of cup are you making?" Suppose the potter had answered with cynical laughter, "Don't be silly. I am not seeking to make any kind of cup in particular. I simply put the clay on the wheel and turn it. If the result is a poem, all right; if it is a monstrosity, all right." Had he made an answer like that he would have shown himself not a wise artist, but a mad bungler.

But we may be sure that this potter is interested in every bit of clay that he seeks to shape into a vessel. Indeed, there is a place where this ugly lump is already a finished product. That is in the mind of the potter. Surely we can expect no less of God! Our Lord is not a mass producer. His interest is always in the individual. He never loses sight of the one among the many. God has dreamed a beautiful dream for every one of us. It is our supreme privilege to make it possible for him to realize that dream.

The fact that God plans every life becomes even more clear in the New Testament. That God planned the life of Jesus is emphasized over and over. "My hour" is a word that was again and again on the lips of our Lord. By this he is affirming that the finger that indicates the hour at which he is to act is that of no human hand, but only that of his Father. He is living constantly within the will of God.

He declares further that God no more planned his life than he did that of his disciples. He affirms that as the Father has sent him, so he was sending these friends. They are to go armed by the same power, girded by the same sense of mission. Since he affirms that God gives to every man his work, we may be sure that he plans our lives as truly as he planned the lives of these disciples of long ago.

II

But the fact that God has a definite will for his world, for every individual, does not mean that his will is always done. "He did what was evil in the sight of the Lord" is affirmed over and over in the lives of these ancient kings. The same may be said of countless millions. None of us will argue with that. It is utterly impossible to imagine a wise and loving God willing all the tragedy that stalks our world today. Indeed it is just our failure to do the will of God that accounts for the vast majority of the heartache, the tears, the disappointed and broken hopes that even now torture so many.

Yet often we hear well-meaning Christians, in seeking to bring comfort to some wounded soul, affirm, "Everything happens for the best." That is, it is all according to the will of God. Of course that is not true at all. There are countless things that, so far as we can see, happen for the worst. Yet having barked our shins against natural law we are prone to peevishly blame God for suffering that we have brought on ourselves.

When I was a pastor in Houston, Texas, a good woman gave her teen-age son a secondhand Ford. He was a reckless driver who delighted in turning curves at high speed in order to hear the tires shriek. One day, as he went shrieking around a curve, a telephone pole met him. He went through the windshield, and if he had not struck the pole with his head it might have killed him. As it was, he was hurried to the hospital. The mother called for the minister; I went at once and found her almost frantic.

She gripped my hands in hers and blurted out this question: "Why should this happen to me?" At the risk of seeming both harsh and flippant, I answered, "It did not happen to you. It happened to him." Then I added, because I saw the need, "Don't blame God for the accident. If God were to snatch a telephone pole from in front of your son when he was driving recklessly, he might put one in front of me when I was driving carefully. In that case nobody would know what to depend upon." All I am arguing for is: let every man hit his own telephone pole; for that is the kind of world we live in, like it or not.

Now, why does not God prevent such accidents? The only true answer is that he cannot. Is he not almighty? He is. But he resigned some of that almightiness when he made you and me. We are the only creatures who can stand at the forks of the road and decide for ourselves whether we shall go to the right or to the left. If we decide upon a right turn, no power in earth or hell can prevent it. If we decide upon a wrong turn, no power in heaven or earth can prevent that. God woos and persuades, but he never compels. "He never poaches upon the sacred precincts of personality."

But does not the Bible affirm over and over that the Lord reigns? Is the shout, "Hallelujah! for the Lord our God the Almighty reigns," only a wistful dream? Not a bit of it. God is on the throne. He is even now King of kings and Lord of lords. But the fact that he is a king does not mean he is a despot. Therefore, the weakest of us have it in our power to resist his will and shut him out of our lives if we so desire. God's will is not always done.

III

But there is this bracing fact. God's will may be done! If this be not true, then the prayer Jesus taught us to pray, "Thy will be done," is sheer mockery. If this be not true, then God is neither loving nor just. For when these kings flouted the will of God, they had to pay a penalty—and the same is true of us. But such a penalty would be unjust if to do the will of God were an impossibility. If it were impossible even by his grace to do his will, then one might stand upon the very floor of the bottomless pit and cry, "Unjust, unjust," until he shook the very foundation of heaven. God's will can be done.

Not only can God's will be done, but it can be done even by failures like ourselves. It can be done by those who up to now have made a mess of their lives. As we, with the prophet, watched the potter at his work, something went wrong. The bit of clay on which he was working failed to become the vessel of his dream. It was marred or spoiled in the making.

So what? I should have expected him to have taken the bit of stubborn clay and to have thrown it away. But this the potter refused to do. Instead he started over again as if that piece of clay were priceless and the only bit he had in the world. Having begun anew, he perhaps failed a second time, a third, a fourth, a thousandth. Even so, he kept right on. He refused to give in till he had realized his dream. Moffatt gives this thrilling translation, "Till he was satisfied."

IV

How then can we know and do the will of God?

It is a fact that God gives to every human soul a sense of right and wrong. Have you ever noticed that almost every man who asked Jesus a question knew the answer before he asked it? When a certain lawyer questioned him as to the first and great commandment, Jesus did not give him the answer. Instead, he threw the question back to the lawyer and let him answer his own question. As that was true of the questions brought to Jesus, it has been true of those brought to me, and I daresay to other ministers. When one comes asking, "Do you think it's wrong to do this or that?" what is generally back of such a question? The conviction on the part of the questioner that it is wrong. They are already sure of the answer. That is the real reason for asking.

There are certain standards of conduct that we all accept. For instance, everyone knows it is better to be sober than to be drunk, better to be clean than to be unclean, better to be courageous than to be a coward. Everyone knows it is better to love than to hate, better to lift than to lean, better to help than to hinder. Everyone knows it is better to give than merely to get, better to be interested in others than to be interested only in ourselves.

Our difficulty is not that we do not know enough; it is rather that we refuse to live up to what we actually know. To walk in the light that is ours is to find fuller light. This is the word of Jesus himself: "If any one is willing to do

His will, he shall know" (Weymouth). That has been tested and found true times without number.

If here and now we should commit ourselves as best we can to the will of God, what would happen? First, he would accept us. What we give he takes. Having accepted us, he would begin at once to remake us. Not only would he remake us, but he would increasingly use and guide us. This does not mean that he would give us a full blueprint of our earthly journey. He would, however, at least make us sure of our next step. It would mean that all of us would be different, increasingly able to do his will according to our individual gifts.

Such dedication might mean for some a call to the ministry. What a rich and rewarding field that is! Having tried it for a little more than half a century, I can recommend it with confidence. So true is this that if I had my life to live over again I would be a minister. Indeed, if I had it to live over a score of times, I would still follow the same high calling, with its laughter and its tears.

If we all were to commit ourselves to the will of God today, some of us might be led to give ourselves to missionary work. It has struck me across the years that our missionaries are about the most wholesome, courageous, joyous, and helpful people whom it has been my privilege to know. The letters of my own son and daughter, who are now medical missionaries in India, are interesting not only because they are full of news, but because they are pervaded by a spirit of gaiety that gives the soul a lift.

God does not have a plan simply for ministers and missionaries and full-time Christian workers; he has a plan for us all. One may be as truly called to serve God as a lawyer, as a physician, as an educator, as a businessman as to serve him as a minister. Therefore, if we all were to enter into the plan of God today, while it would bring radical changes for some, such would not be the case for the majority. Most of us would go on with our same daily rounds, but there would be this difference. We would do all this under brighter and roomier skies. Because each of us, whether great or small, could look up from his task and say, "To this end was I born, and for this cause came I into the world."

What then supremely matters? There is only one answer to that question. It is the will of God. If we flout the will of God, nothing can bring us to our best in time or in eternity. If we accept the will of God, nothing can ultimately defeat us in time or eternity. When, therefore, these writers say, "He did what was right in the eyes of the Lord," or "He did what was evil in the sight of the Lord," they are telling us that which is supremely important for every human soul, whether king or slave.

II. THE SKYROCKET (SAUL)

> *"Do you see him whom the Lord has choosen? There is none like him among all the people." And all the people shouted, "Long live the king!"*
>
> —I SAM. 10:24
>
> *Therefore Saul took his own sword, and fell upon it.*
>
> —I SAM. 31:5

There are those who inspire and thrill us by their great returns from meager gifts. They make so much of so little. I am thinking of a queer chap born in a one-room log cabin with a dirt floor, far back in our mountains. He was heavily handicapped physically. He was also totally lacking in formal education. But in his middle twenties, through a mighty conversion, he became a dedicated man. One day I dared to invite him to preach to my people in a large city church. I have seldom seen any congregation more deeply moved. He had so little, yet by the grace of God he made so much of it.

Saul impresses us in the opposite direction. He had so much and made so little of it. What gifts he had! What a brilliant start he made! He sprang suddenly from obscurity into the radiance of royalty. His ascent was as dazzling as that of a blazing skyrocket. But all too soon the light went out and what gave promise of so much splendor ended in darkness and utter night. Saul took great gifts and all but threw them away.

I

Look at his assets.

1. He was blessed with a fine physical body. That is no mean gift. There was a time when certain saints viewed the body with critical eyes. To them it was not an ally but an enemy. We have come to a far saner view, however: The body is not our foe; it is our friend. It is the house in which we are to live so long as we work in this world. It is the car we are to drive, at least to the gates of the cemetery. We might be able to make the journey both joyfully and helpfully in a tumbledown jalopy. But our chances would certainly be better in a well-kept Cadillac. Our bodies are something sacred—as sacred as our souls. Indeed, they are temples of the Holy Spirit.

It would seem then that Saul kept his fine body clean. The Israelites of his day practiced polygamy. The kings who succeeded Saul generally gave themselves to a veritable orgy of marrying. Had Solomon decided to visit any American city and take all his wives with him, he would have had great difficulty in finding any hotel large enough to accommodate them. But so far as the record goes, it would seem that Saul clung to the wife of his youth to the end of the day. He possessed a strong clean body.

2. Saul was courageous. As a soldier he never flinched. In his fits of madness he was dogged by fear, but this was not native to him. He went bravely against the enemy when he was undergirded by some sense of God and by bracing hopes of victory. But he was no less courageous when hope was gone, and when he knew his only reward would be dishonor and death when the battle came to an end. He was a man of courage.

3. Saul was amazingly generous. No sooner had he been crowned than he had to meet opposition. He was despised by some who had perhaps known him as a farm boy. They could not understand on what strange meat this young Caesar had fed that he had grown so strong. Therefore, they ridiculed him and made his position as hard as possible.

Soon their laughter was changed to terror, however. Saul returned, flushed with victory, from his first encounter with the enemy. His friends, therefore, went at once to Samuel demanding the death penalty for these scoffers. I am not sure this prophet did not agree. But not so Saul. With a beautiful generosity he declared that God had given them a great victory and that he was not going to spoil that victory by staining it with the blood of vengeance. He was amazingly generous.

4. Saul was also beautifully humble. When Samuel told him of his great destiny he did not accept the news as a matter of course. Instead he reminded the prophet that he

belonged to the smallest tribe of all Israel—and further, that his family was obscure even in that tribe. When they were ready to put the crown on his brow, he was hiding from greatness. Those called to positions of honor either in church or state generally keep themselves in sight. More amazing still, when his uncle questioned him as to what the prophet had said to him, Saul made no mention of the fact that he had been called to be king. Had such an event happened to me, I fear I would have laid all but violent hands upon the first stranger I met, asking, "Did you know that I am going to be king?"

Some years ago a circuit rider in Texas had to give up his ministry because of a weak throat. He became a tenant farmer, renting land from a wealthy rancher. This ranchman soon came to trust his tenant. Often he had him bring large sums of money from the village bank for the payroll.

This fact became known, and one evening, as he was nearing home, a highwayman stepped from among the mesquite trees and pointed a gun in his face. "You have five thousand dollars," he said. "I want it." The preacher answered, "Yes, I have five thousand dollars, but I am not going to give it to you. We are alone. If I should give you this money I could never prove that we were not partners. I have nothing to leave my family except this wagon and team and my good name. Therefore, I am not going to give you the money. If you want it badly enough to kill me, go ahead. You will get it in no other way." At that the highwayman uttered an oath, turned on his heels, and disappeared.

Later this robber held up another man and committed murder. He was caught, tried, and sentenced to death. When asked if he desired the visit of a minister before his execution he answered in the affirmative. The man for whom he asked was the tenant farmer. "Why him?" they inquired in amazement. "He doesn't even have a church." Then the doomed man told his story. And the tremendous fact is that the preacher himself had never told it. What a man! He possessed, even more than did Saul, the virtue of humility.

5. Finally, Saul was God's choice. Why? Certainly God did not choose him because he was perfect—he was very far from it. With all his fine qualities he was ever a man of timid faith. Till the time of his meeting with Samuel he seems to have had no religion at all. It is a rather startling fact that although Samuel was far the best-known man in all Israel, Saul not only had never met him but had not even heard of him. Saul's servant had to tell him both the prophet's name and city.

This means that when Samuel had preached to the tribe of Benjamin, Saul did not attend. I think he failed to because his father, Kish, did not attend. Years ago at a state fair the hog that took the prize was being cared for by a boy who was about the poorest specimen to be found. Yet the man who raised the prize hog was letting the boy grow up without proper attention. I have an idea that Kish was more interested in livestock than in the religious training of his son. Be that as it may, Saul was still God's choice because he was the best man in sight.

II

In spite of Saul's great gifts, his career is a disappointment. Although he had come to some kind of religious experience at his anointing, he was never deeply dedicated. Nor was it easy for him to get on with his famous pastor, Samuel. It would seem that they seldom saw eye to eye. Somehow they had a way of getting on each other's nerves. They had two rather shocking encounters after Saul had become king. In the first I think they were both somewhat at fault. In the other encounter the fault was Saul's.

The first encounter was by agreement. Saul and Samuel were to meet at a certain place at a certain hour so that Samuel might offer sacrifice on the eve of a pending battle. But for some reason the preacher was late. Why, we are not told, but my guess is that he had no good reason. There are those who are constitutionally late. There are those who can get in a traffic jam when they are the only ones on the street. Being late was Samuel's way of saying to Saul, "My time is important but yours is of no value at all."

Now this lateness on the part of the prophet was very disturbing. The soldiers, unwilling to go to battle without a sacrifice, were beginning to desert. Saul found himself in a tight corner; therefore he decided to offer the sacrifice himself. Of course he knew that for him this was wrong, but he justified it because this was an emergency. He had hardly finished when the prophet showed up. Realizing what Saul had done, Samuel was outraged.

I am willing to believe that a part of his anger might have been righteous indignation, but it was not wholly so, for Samuel had never desired a king of any kind. When the people had asked for a king he had been angry because they had repudiated him. And his anger had come out in the words, "Far be it from me that I should sin against the Lord by ceasing to pray for you." That means that in his anger he had decided to quit praying for them altogether.

Now, however, having become reconciled in some measure to the loss of his civil power, he felt that Saul was seeking to become priest as well. Therefore in anger he rebuked him sharply and strongly hinted that his dynasty would not last.

In my opinion, in this unfortunate encounter Samuel was as much to blame as the king. But such was not the case with their next—here the fault was Saul's alone. He had been sent on a mission—what was once known as a "holy war." Of course, we have since discovered that war is generally about as holy as hell. But this expedition was in the nature of a surgical operation. A certain tribe was to be destroyed, along with everything it possessed. The destruction of property was to rescue the enterprise from the stain of being a mere robbery by violence. Saul executed his mission—but only so far as it suited him. He killed off the worthless stock but kept the prize sheep and cattle. He also brought back King Agag. This he did, not for reasons of mercy, but in order to have a king to dance attendance upon him.

That night the word of the Lord came to Samuel, saying, "He [Saul] has turned back from following after me." Then, after a night of prayer, Samuel came to see Saul. The king greeted him with this pious word: "Blessed be you to the Lord; I have performed the commandment of the

Lord." Then it was that some very thoughtless sheep and impolite oxen dared to give Saul the lie. "What then," questioned the preacher, "is this bleating of the sheep in my ears, and the lowing of the oxen which I hear?"

Thus the king was caught. But instead of facing up to it honestly, he passed the buck. He said the people did it. And not only that, but they did it for a religious reason. They brought the sheep and cattle along to sacrifice to the Lord. Samuel, in his reply, is at his best:

Has the Lord as great delight in burnt offerings and sacrifices,
as in obeying the voice of the Lord?
Behold, to obey is better than sacrifice,
and to hearken than the fat of rams.

God never sells indulgences at any price, whether in terms of money or service.

Then it was that the prophet pronounced his ruthless sentence against Saul. He told him that because he had rejected God, God had rejected him from being king. Saul then confessed his sin and begged the prophet to forgive him and to honor him at least in the presence of the people. He did not deeply care for the wrong he had done, but he did care deeply for the penalty it had brought.

After this experience, Saul's sun gradually went into eclipse. He and Samuel met no more. He seems never to have had any dealings with any other priests. Without priestly guidance, without any sense of God, he became subject to fits of depressions. Black moods gripped him more and more and plunged him into a night so bitter as to be akin to madness. Then a remedy for these black moods was found in the person of a brilliant poet and singer by the name of David. But even this remedy ended by becoming more torturing than the disease.

When David first came on the scene, Saul was charmed. But what boded ill for Saul was that everyone else was charmed, too. Besides, this young shepherd was more than a poet; he was also a soldier.

One day, as Saul was coming with David from a victorious battle, some foolish girls met them with this song:

> Saul has slain his thousands,
> And David his ten thousands.

Thus the subject was made ten times greater than the king. Had Saul not resented that he would have been more than human. Increasingly he gave way to jealousy and hate till he came to nurse murder in his heart. Naturally that plunged him into a living hell. He was dead wrong of course, but what great provocation was his!

At last came the final scene. Saul was once more surrounded by his old enemies, the Philistines. He was desperate. He needed help, but he knew not where to turn. "God has turned away from me," he sobbed, "and answers me no more." Then in his utter desperation he turned to a medium, a kind of creature whom he had once despised.

That scene in Endor is not easy to explain; but it would seem that God spoke to Saul once more, not through this medium, but through Samuel whom Saul somehow could not love and with whom he had broken. The prophet gave a message of doom, the only one that he could give under the circumstances. Thus Saul went out to battle the next day armed only with the certainty of disaster. With grim courage he saw the long day through. Then, when his brave sons had fallen about him, when everything was lost, he asked his armor-bearer to thrust him through. Naturally the man was afraid. "Therefore Saul took his own sword, and fell upon it."

How much he had! How utterly he threw it away!

III

What was the matter with Saul? He is, in many respects, one of the most bewildering characters of the Bible. As I have tried to live with him and watch him in action, I have come to the conviction that he had this fundamental defect. He was never 100 per cent decisive. He lacked out-and-outness. He never attained that wholeheartedness which made his successor David so pleasing both to God and to man. He seemed unable to go all out for any high choice.

For instance, when sent on this mission of extermination, he performed it—but only in part. He was perfectly willing to destroy what he did not value. He was willing to give up that which was not worth keeping. But he refused to give up what he desired for himself. Even so, we are often willing to give up certain glaring and shocking sins that do not appeal to us, while we cling to others that are more pleasing and respectable. Or we are glad to do certain tasks, to shoulder certain responsibilities provided they are popular and pleasing, while we repudiate others that are difficult and unpopular.

Now when Samuel showed Saul that a half obedience was a whole disobedience, he confessed his sin. Indeed, Saul was the greatest confessor that we meet on the pages of the Bible. That is a blessed word which declares: "If we confess our sins, he is faithful and just, and will forgive our sins and cleanse us from all unrighteousness." I think I have used that to lead more seekers to Christ than any other passage in the Bible. Why, then, did not Saul find this cleansing? The answer is that in his repentance, as in his obedience, he was always halfhearted. Though constantly confessing his sins, he refused utterly to forsake them and to turn wholeheartedly to him who is able to forgive.

This habit of halfheartedness weakens and paralyzes Saul to the very end. On grim Gilboa, when all hope was gone, fearing that he might fall into the hands of the enemy, he was eager to die. He desired to commit suicide, and yet at the same time not to commit suicide. Therefore he asked death at the hands of his armor-bearer. It was only when this request was refused that he fell on his sword.

But for the fact that Saul was constantly of a divided mind, he might have been one of the greatest kings Israel ever had. Yet in spite of so much that was fine in him, his lack of decisiveness cost him his throne, his usefulness—his very all.

III. THE UNCROWNED KING (JONATHAN)

You shall be king over Israel, and I shall be next to you.

—I SAM. 23:17

These are the words of David's friend Jonathan. He was Saul's eldest son and heir to the throne of Israel. But he never reached that throne, and never wore a crown. Yet, as we read his story, we are more and more convinced that a crown for him was not necessary. He was kingly in himself. He was so full of charm, so full of faith, so full of courage, so full of the choicest of virtues, that no crown could have been an ornament to him. In fact, the most resplendent diadem would have looked like mere tinsel on that royal brow. He is one of the most winsome personalities in the pages of the Bible.

I want to present him to you in the three crises in his life.

I

When first we meet him he is with his father in the field against the Philistines. The Hebrew people at that time were in a bad way. Their fortunes were at about the lowest possible ebb. Some of them had deserted to the foe. Others were hiding in dens and caves in the hills, afraid to show their faces. Some six hundred ill-armed chaps were with their royal master, Saul. These were still in the open but totally without heart to face the garrison of the enemy that was very close at hand. Thus, they were spending the days in idle fear and humiliating waiting.

Jonathan, however, decided that he would act. He did not take his father into his confidence. I think he did this because he feared that his father would object. Be that as it may, Jonathan reached the conclusion that almost any action would be better than inaction. He took his decision not recklessly, but girded by this firm faith, "Nothing can hinder the Lord from saving by many or by few." For those ancient Hebrews all wars were holy wars. Convinced of this, Jonathan went to the attack assured that it was not the might of his sword that counted, but the might of God who enabled him to wield that sword.

So with no help but that of his armor-bearer, he gave challenge to the Philistines. Naturally these Philistines were overconfident. I think they regarded the young prince as a bit of a joke. Therefore, they invited him to meet them, but Jonathan chose the place of meeting. It was a narrow passage between two rugged crags where only one or two men could stand abreast. Meeting the Philistines on these terms, he succeeded in killing about a score of them. The rest were thrown into panic. Not only so, but since there is nothing more contagious than cowardice, they made the whole camp panic. Soon the Philistines were running as for their hunted lives.

This created such a tumult that Saul saw what was happening and, with his ill-equipped army, started in pursuit. These were joined by the one-time deserters. Then even those shirkers who had been hiding among the hills swarmed out of their caves and with a shout swaggered after a fleeing foe. Thus heroes, deserters, and shirkers joined in pursuit of an already defeated enemy, and there was a great victory. But that victory was really won by a one-man army named Jonathan.

There was one blot upon this victory, however. Saul had that day made a rash vow that no one should taste any food until the day was over. He had the idea that has haunted religious people through the centuries—that God is pleased if we make ourselves miserable. Now to sacrifice for a purpose is noble, but to sacrifice just for the sake of sacrificing has nothing of nobleness about it. Those saints of the Middle Ages who forsook the world and whipped themselves both for penance and discipline may have deserved the whipping, but their suffering did not help anything, not even themselves.

It so happened that Jonathan knew nothing of this silly vow. Therefore, when he came upon some honey he ate it. Not only so, but he encouraged the fainting soldiers to eat. This he did more by his conduct than by his words. He knew that a soldier could fight better on a full stomach than on an empty one. Then, too, I think he had a keen interest in the welfare of his soldiers. He was therefore eager to relieve their hunger.

But Saul took far too harsh a view of Jonathan's conduct. "Tell me what you have done," he questioned. "I tasted a little honey," was the reply. Then Saul passed upon him the sentence of death. How did Jonathan react?

He did not tell his half-mad father that he was foolish for making such a vow. He did not remind him that it was due solely to the victory that he had won that Saul was now able to carry out his stupid vow. But with a devotion and loyalty to his father that never wavered though so greatly strained, he said with beautiful humility and courage, "Here I am, I will die."

The soldiers would not have it, however. With high courage, they declared, "There shall not one hair of his head fall to the ground." Thus, wiser than Saul, they showed their appreciation of the fact that Jonathan had brought them a victory such as they had not experienced for many a gloomy day.

II

We get our second view of this gallant prince as Saul—once more with an inadequate army—faced the Philistines. This time it was decided to settle the contest in about the most humane way. A champion was to be chosen by each side and the one who won was to bring victory to the whole army. That was better than our highly civilized methods where we kill not only soldiers but civilians and little children as well. Now the challenger for the Philistines was a huge, rugged chap named Goliath. (He reminds me considerably of a gentleman of our day—a gallant, shoe-pounding hero called Khrushchev.) Goliath, of course, was a little more refined. But he was still a bully as he challenged the Israelites to send a foe against whom he could display his power.

Then one day, when he was making his oft-repeated challenge, it so happened that there was a young shepherd present whose name was David. When he heard this challenge, his eyes flashed and his cheeks glowed. He watched with breathless excitement to see a mad scramble on the part of all the soldiers to claim the honor of facing this giant. To his utter amazement, not a man volunteered. Even when he himself showed a live interest, his oldest brother rebuked him with scorn, sneering, "Why have you come down? And with whom have you left those few sheep?" But this youth was not to be daunted, even by his older brother. So he took the matter up with the king.

Why, I wonder, had not Jonathan accepted this challenge? I have an idea it was because of his too-cautious father. And further, I have an idea that Jonathan was not present when David volunteered. Jonathan and his father were very close. They consulted each other about all important matters. Since Jonathan's name is not mentioned here, I imagine he was absent. But if he was absent when David went out to the conflict, he was present when he returned a victor. He saw him as with the stride of a conqueror he returned, bringing the head of the giant in his hand.

What was Jonathan's reaction? What would have been the reaction of a lesser man?

Some time ago, during a great campaign being conducted by Billy Graham, I am told that a certain minister, pastor of one of the largest churches of that city, made the gallant announcement: "I could conduct meetings such as Graham is conducting if I wanted to." Well, perhaps he could. Yet such a statement, I am persuaded, did not add one cubit to his stature. Instead, it gave the impression that he might be a bit of a dwarf.

Jonathan did not react in that way. Instead, he was fairly swept off his feet with enthusiasm. His eyes sparkled, his face became radiant, and his heart was all aglow. He looked upon David with boundless admiration. He saw in him a hero bigger and braver than himself. Therefore, the story tells us that the soul of Jonathan was knit to the soul of David and that he loved him as he loved himself.

That knitting of soul to soul was possible because these two had so much in common. They could be thus welded together because they were kindred metals. It is not easy to weld gold to clay. Hosea tried it when he sought to weld the clay soul of Gomer to his own golden soul. But it did not work. With these two, however, who had so much in common, it did work. For this reason there began here one of the most beautiful friendships of all history.

Now the one most responsible for this friendship was Jonathan. His friendship for David was far more costly than David's to himself. Indeed, by this friendship David was to gain everything, but Jonathan was to give everything. In that his friendship resembles that of our Lord who said, "No longer do I call you servants . . . ; but I have called you friends." He has come to be our friend, and in so doing he puts into this friendship all that he has. "All that is mine is yours." How much must we put into it? Naturally, if we are to receive his all, we must give our all. This we should do gladly. He has infinite to give while we have only our small selves.

There was a king in our day who gave up a throne for the woman he loved. Now I am not questioning the sincerity of his love. I cannot, however, give it quite 100 per cent of my confidence. This is because I have an idea that he had a strong hope that his people would not permit his giving up the crown. But be that as it may, he did give it up. How much did the woman in the case give? We cannot know. But as I see it, she gained everything while the king gave everything. "The only way to have a friend," said Emerson, "is to be one." David, therefore, must have given grandly. But Jonathan's giving was greater still. He gave his very all.

III

The last crisis I mention has to do with the two final meetings of these devoted friends. At the first of these David said to Jonathan—with what seems to me a touch of suspicion—"There is but a step between me and death." I am inclined to think that at first David had suspected that Jonathan knew about this threat to his life on the part of Saul, and was taking sides with his father. David further said to Jonathan that it is not *we* who have now entered into covenant before God together, but you (Jonathan) who have entered into a covenant with me before God. Here I think David falls far short of Jonathan. He was a great friend, but he was not quite equal in this to princely

Jonathan whose loyalty and self-giving love nothing could shake.

Listen to this: "And Jonathan, Saul's son, rose, and went to David . . . and strengthened his hand in God." What a Christlike visit that was! How deeply and beautifully unselfish! Jonathan was afraid that his friend, whose youthful brow had already been anointed, might fail in his faith and, thus failing, miss the crown. He was determined that should not happen. This was the case in spite of the fact that he knew if David were to let the crown slip, it would then be his own. Thus this prince knew that in order for him to win he would not have to "wade through slaughter to a throne." All he would have to do was nothing. In spite of this he went the limit to uncrown himself for the sake of his friend.

IV

Now why did Jonathan take this amazing course? Why did he deliberately renounce his crown? I am sure he did not do it because he was too sluggish to care. Nor did he do it because he was interested neither in serving his people nor in being honored by them. There are some things we give up simply because we do not care for them. But such was not the case here.

I qualify as a good fisherman. I not only catch fish, but I catch choice fish—the smallmouth, swift-water bass. But having caught them, I usually give them to my friends. And the further tragedy is that I feel sure that these friends do not greatly appreciate them because they, knowing that I do not eat fish, realize that my gift is not sacrificial.

Had I met Esau the day after he sold his birthright I would have seen no tears on his face. Had I said to him in deepest sympathy, "Esau, I'm so sorry! It breaks my heart that you have had to part from your birthright," Esau would have burst into wild laughter and said, "Don't waste any tears on me. I was hungry. I couldn't eat a birthright, so I gave it for something I could get my teeth into." He came to be sorry in later years, but it was no sacrifice then for him to give up his birthright; he did not care for it.

But how about Jonathan? Did he care for the crown? Did he have any patriotism? Was he eager to please his father whose dearest dream was to leave him a throne? He cared immensely. We can be sure of this because he cared enough for his country to die for it. He cared enough for his father to die with and for him. They fell side by side on that bloody hill of Gilboa. Greater love has no man than this, that he will lay down his life for his father and for his country. But in spite of that love—and because of that love—Jonathan resigned the crown in favor of David.

He did this because he loved David with a love that seeks not its own. But there was more in his love than mere fondness. It is often said that love is blind. Perhaps—but the opposite is also true. It is the most keen-eyed thing in the world. It can see sparkling jewels where others can see only paste. Jonathan did not give up the crown only to put it on the brow of one who was worthless. He believed in David with all his soul. He believed that this divinely anointed friend would make a better king even than he himself could make.

This does not mean that Jonathan suffered from an inferiority complex. He was too wholesome and great for that. Yet, though he knew he could make a strong and wise king, he believed that his friend would make a better one. Therefore he put David first, not solely because he was seeking the best for his friend, but because he was seeking the best for God's people. Whatever was for their highest good, he was willing at all cost to do. Thus Jonathan's giving was not only a gift born of love; it was also a gift of a profound and vital faith, both in his friend and in his God.

A gentleman told me some time ago of the reply of his minister when he chided him for his seemingly foolish habit of seeking somebody else to play before the footlights while he himself played backstage. "Why, man," he answered simply, "I'm out for the cause. Whatever helps the cause of my Lord is the prize on which I set my eye. Therefore if I find a man who is one inch taller in ability than I am, I'll put him out ahead. I'll hold his coat and run his errands. I'm not out to shine. I'm out to get the work done." That was like Jonathan. That was supremely like our Lord.

> What matter, I or they?
> Mine or another's day,
> So the right word be said
> And life the sweeter made?
> —JOHN GREENLEAF WHITTIER, "My Triumph"

Here, then, is one who lived centuries ago in a grim and cruel age. Yet of all the characters we meet on the pages of the Bible, I know few indeed who impress me as more Christlike than this great friend, this great believer, this great giver, this uncrowned king—Jonathan.

IV. A ROYAL CRIMINAL (DAVID)

The sword slays one as well as another.
—II SAM. 11:25 (MOFFATT)

"The sword slays one as well as another." What a self-evident and commonplace truth that is! Upon hearing that, nobody is tempted to rise in angry protest. Yet heard aright, what a damning and loathsome lie! David has just committed about the ugliest crime recorded on the pages of the Bible. But here he descends to yet deeper depths by pleading not guilty. "Sure Uriah is dead, but I am in no sense to blame. He was a victim of the fortunes of war. The sword slays one as well as another." Thus, this royal criminal sounded the lowest depths and—for the moment at least—slammed the door of hope in his own face.

I

How did this deeply religious king, who had feared the Lord from his youth, come to be guilty of this hideous crime? Of course we know that his first step down was the sin of adultery. This ugly deed was made the more hideous by the fact that the woman in the case was the wife of a faithful and honored soldier. This soldier was away at the time fighting for the king who was wrecking his home. The base ingratitude, the utter lack of loyalty, either to God or to man, that lay back of that fall could hardly be exaggerated. No wonder it put David's feet on a toboggan where there was no stopping till he reached the very bottom.

This temptation came upon David in an hour of idleness. How many of us go wrong for lack of something better to do! When I was a boy certain Sunday-school teachers used to tell us that work was sent us as a curse. That is, if Adam and Eve had only behaved themselves as they should, then everybody could have lived off the government instead of just half of the people as in our day.

But, of course, work is not a curse. It is one of life's supreme blessings. It is a means of growth, a roadway to self-respect. It is a great safeguard against temptation. When sturdy Nehemiah was being invited to a council that would have meant the death of him, he stood firm by being able to make this assertion: "I am doing a great work and I cannot come down." David could no longer say that. He was then residing in a house of idleness whose open doors always invite temptation.

> It was not in the open fight
> We threw away the sword,
> But in the lonely watching
> In the darkness by the ford.
> The waters lapped, the night-wind blew,
> Full-armed the Fear was born and grew,

And we were flying ere we knew
From panic in the night.[1]

Then David had reached that prosaic period we call middle age. We have many sermons for youth, quite a few for the aged, but almost none for those who are braving the middle passage. Yet this is the group that makes up most of our congregations. It is also the group that is carrying the heaviest part of the world's load. It is this group also that is peculiarly tempted. Possibly more people go irretrievably wrong in this middle passage of life than in any other.

It is easy to see why this is the case. Youth tends to be idealistic. Youth sees visions and dreams dreams. But by the time we reach middle age we have run past many of our ideals. We have become slaves to the practical. We have allowed the potatoes to displace the roses. We are too far from the morning to be romantic but not close enough to the eventide to be softened by the thought of going home.

One spring day some months ago I watched a young ant making his first venture into the sunlight. He had wings. He spurned the ground as if he would seek the sky. But very soon he lost all interest in the heights and soared no more. Instead he said, "Business is business." Then he threw away his wings and began to crawl.

In Tennyson's Round Table story, a young man named Gareth is seeking to win knighthood. But before he can

[1] "The Rout of the White Hussars by Rudyard Kipling from the book *Plain Tales from the Hills.* Reprinted by permission of Doubleday & Company, Inc., The Macmillan Company of Canada, Ltd., and Mrs. George Bambridge.

attain his goal, he must meet and conquer certain foes. First is the Knight of the Morning Star; second is the Knight of the Noonday Sun. David also met these two knights. He won grandly his battle with the Knight of the Morning Star. His youthful victory over Goliath, a victory of faith over force, is an abidingly gripping story. But this same hero went down in utter defeat before the Knight of the Noonday Sun. Indeed there is a destruction that wasteth at noonday. Few are in greater peril than the man who is sure that he has arrived. Such men especially need to pray this great prayer, "Revive thy work in the midst of the years, in the midst of the years make known" (K.J.V.).

David had a false sense of security. Part of this security perhaps was the outcome of the self-sufficiency born of his great success. His every undertaking had ended in victory. Human hearts had opened to him as flowers at the kiss of spring. He felt he could get away with anything. I used to know a young chap like that. He had a personality as winning as a baby's smile. By and by, with a kind of swagger, he became a drug addict. As such he would sometimes tell me how he could spot an addict a block away. But all the while he was blissfully sure that nobody could spot him. Then the inevitable crash came.

David felt secure not only because of his confidence in himself, but because he was so sure that no one need ever know. He had all the agencies of despotic power to protect him. There seemed not the slightest danger of exposure. Therefore he could have his fling and nobody need be the wiser. So braced by a false sense of security he took the plunge.

II

What was the outcome?

He quickly found that his security was a sham. No sooner had he done this secret wrong than fear began to yap at his heels. Every evil we do secretly always involves fear. Ours is a day in which the sin of adultery is regarded with shocking tolerance. So much is this the case that when one man asked a certain cynic for the time of day, he answered, "It's sex o'clock." But with all that, even this sin requires secrecy and for that reason still turns loose the nemeses of fear upon the guilty.

At first the baying of the hound of fear seemed to David quite distant and all but harmless. But when the woman in the case whispered that a new life was on the way, then this guilty king could almost feel the hot breath of the pursuing hound upon his neck. Thus, tortured by fear, he knew that something had to be done. He simply could not bear the shame of having it known that he had so desperately wronged a gallant officer of his army and so sinned against his God.

It was then that he became a creature of shifts and shams. With brazen hypocrisy he sent to call Uriah to a conference. When Uriah came David, with pretended sincerity, asked him about Joab, about his fellow soldiers, about the progress of the war. Then, the conference over, he ordered Uriah to go down to his own home for the night.

But it so happened that this soldier was a man of superb loyalty and devotion. Therefore, realizing that his comrades were sleeping in the open, deprived of the comforts of home, he refused such comforts for himself. So he slept that night before the king's door. The next day David discovered that he had not gone to his own home. Therefore, he was still more disturbed. The torture of fear was still more agonizing.

Then he made a final effort. He sought to get Uriah drunk. He knew even then that liquor has a way of killing all inhibitions, that it tends to blind one to all moral distinctions. Surely, he reasoned, a drunk Uriah would have no scruples about accepting privileges denied to his fellow soldiers. But in spite of the king's efforts Uriah did not get drunk enough to outrage his convictions.

Then what? The ghastly thought of putting Uriah out of the way came to the king. I think at first it made him shudder. "Not murder," he said with horror. Next he began to toy with the thought, to rationalize about it. Then suddenly it dawned on him that he could kill Uriah and not kill him at the same time. What a fine scheme! So Uriah was again called before the king. David, with a fine show of friendship, put the loyal soldier's death warrant in his hands and sent him back to Joab.

This death warrant was in the form of a little note from the king himself. It ordered Joab to make an attack on the city, put Uriah in the front, then withdraw from him so that his death at the hand of the enemy would be a certainty. And thus it was done. Then, this royal criminal, having plunged into the abyss of murder, crowned it all with this ghastly lie, "I am in no sense to blame. The sword slays one as well as another." It would be hard to find an uglier crime than that.

III

Yet this royal criminal was forgiven.

How did it come about? The first move, of course, was God's. That is ever the case. Once we have made a wrong choice, he never allows us to be fully at peace. The very pangs of hell got hold of David. There is no measuring what this once saintly man suffered—the agony of guilt, the even more appalling anguish of a lost sense of God. The Good Shepherd whom David once knew no longer led him. Instead, he was lost in a wilderness as torturing as hell.

Then David was helped by human hands. God in his wisdom and mercy has a way of reaching me through you, or you through me. There is no sharper test of our dedication, I think, than our willingness to go to a friend who has lost the way and confront him personally with the claims of our Lord. To me, at least, it has never been easy. Yet as I have gone with fear and trembling, how often I have found that the Lord had gone ahead and prepared the way. Sometimes we have the feeling that our friend was simply waiting for our invitation.

What dedication it took on the part of Nathan to pay this pastoral visit to his king! None of us relish rebukes, least of all one like David who was accustomed to the opposite. But Nathan took his life in his hands and went. He was very tactful; he told the king a story of rank injustice. David was outraged. How much uglier is the sin *you* have committed than when it is committed by *me!* "The man who has done this deserves to die," said David in anger. He was eager to do something decent in order to bring some bit of healing to his wounded self-respect.

Then the bolt struck. "You are the man," said the prophet. I heard a brother minister preach on this text years ago. He declared that Nathan shook his finger in David's face and thundered at him. Of course his guess is as good as mine. But judging by the outcome I do not think it happened that way at all. I rather think that the prophet said in a voice choked with sobs, "Your Majesty, it breaks my heart to say it, but you are the man."

Then what? Instead of being a creature of shifts and devices and answering, "Thou canst not say I did it; never shake thy gory locks at me," David's knees went weak and he sobbed out this prayer:

> Have mercy on me, O God,
> according to thy steadfast love;
> according to thy abundant mercy
> blot out my transgressions.
> . . . .
> wash me, and I shall be whiter than snow.

That prayer God answered—he always does. For it is forever true that if we confess our sins, he is faithful and just, and will forgive our sins and cleanse us from all unrighteousness.

Along with this radiant ending, however, there is a solemn warning. God did save David from his sin, but what he did not do and could not do was save him from the consequences of his sin. The prophet Nathan told him that the sword would not depart from his house. That sword pierced his heart through the sins of his own children. The agony of that grim experience was even more terrible because he had to say to himself, "You are to blame." God will forgive our wild-oat sowing, but even his forgiveness will not save us from reaping some bit of the harvest.

Some time ago I was called to see a vigorous young woman who was dying of bichloride of mercury poisoning, self-administered. Of all ways to shuffle off, that, I think, is the most ghastly—unless one takes enough to kill quickly. She had not done that, and so she was dying by the inch.

As she gripped my hand in both of hers, she said, "I have sent for you to ask you just one question. I want an honest answer." I said, "I will answer your question to the very best of my ability." "This," she said, "is the question. I have taken my own life. Will God forgive me?"

I was so glad to have a gospel of infinite mercy. "Surely he will," I said with assurance. "There is no sin that our Lord will not forgive. 'He was wounded for our transgressions, he was bruised for our iniquities; upon him was the chastisement that made us whole, and with his stripes we are healed.' " I think she went out in the peace of that healing. But there is one thing that divine healing did not do for her; it did not take the poison out of her veins.

There is no sin, even the most ghastly, that our Lord will not forgive if only we repent. But since repentance does not always save us, and those who are bound in a bundle of life with us, from the consequences, our supreme wisdom is to repent before we become guilty.

V. THE SHEPHERD KING (DAVID)

I took you from the pasture, from following the sheep, that you should be prince over my people Israel.

—II SAM. 7:8

While I was a student at Harvard I went to one of the Boston theaters to see a play that ran for about one hundred nights. The name of that play was *The Shepherd King.* The hero, David, was played by the author, Wright Lorimer. He was a brilliant and idealistic young man who took his art seriously. Perhaps the play did not possess all the merit it had in my eyes. I was young and quite lacking in experience. But be that as it may, I was thrilled and enchanted. For that brief hour I lived in a new world redolent of romance and poetry and also of high faith. This shepherd king cast a spell over me that night from which I have never fully recovered.

Why should this not have been the case? As a success story Horatio Alger never wrote one that comes within leagues of it. *From Shepherd's Tent to Royal Palace*—what a title that would make for a best seller! But the story of the shepherd king is far more than a glittering picture of getting on. It is far more than a record of a military genius who waded through slaughter to a throne. It is the story of a man, intensely human, whose name has yet become, in a sense, a part of that of our Lord. Centuries later a blind beggar found sight through this prayer "Jesus, Son of David, have mercy on me!"

I

David was a many-sided man. There are those who are greatly gifted in one direction, but who have meager gifts in another. There are those who are lopsided—half-baked. But this shepherd king was symmetrical. He was well rounded. God seems to have given him almost every gift.

Physically, he was a bit of a poem. As a rule the writers of the Bible are not greatly concerned with outward appearances. They are sure that while man looks on the outward appearance, God looks on the heart. They do not even give us a description of the physical appearance of our Lord. But they feel compelled to describe David. We are told of his lovely complexion. What a hit he would have made on television, advertising cosmetics! The author tells us further of the beauty of his eyes. He was an all-around handsome man. It was doubtless from him that his son Absalom inherited the good looks that so inflated him as to help toward his own undoing. David was gifted physically.

Then, he was richly endowed with a virtue that all admire; that is courage. He had physical courage to a high degree. Better still, he had moral courage as well. When he volunteered to meet Goliath, that required great physical courage. But even more terrifying than fighting this giant was the ordeal of facing his own people. In doing this he had to brave the sneers of his elder brother as he scornfully inquired about his few sheep. He had to dare also the gloomy questionings of Saul. Perhaps harder still, he had to face the bewildered glances of the common soldiers, who, though eager to call him a hero, felt compelled to call him a fool. Thus, David had the fine courage to trust himself when all men doubted and to "make allowance for their doubting too."

David was a man of vast intellectual ability. The author tells us that he was quick-witted; that is, he had an alert and sparkling mind. He tells us also that, though a rustic, he behaved himself wisely in the royal court. Nor was he simply a brilliant nitwit; he was a thoroughly practical man. He possessed that sense without which, we are told, all other sense is nonsense: He had commonsense.

Thus gifted, he became an able and victorious military leader. He was also an equally wise and practical statesman. He knew how to rule. So wisely did he govern that his people through all the centuries have looked back to his reign as their golden age. Not only this, but as his reign was their most bracing memory, so the expectation of the reign of his greater Son was looked forward to as their fondest hope.

This warrior statesman was a prophet and poet. His prophetic utterances are frequently quoted in the New Testament, especially by our Lord. He also had a flock of songbirds in his heart. He early became leader of the Marine

Band. In fact, he was the band himself. Perhaps he sang some of his first psalms to quiet the ravings of half-mad Saul.

Just how many of the psalms attributed to David are really his it is impossible to say. The very fact, however, that he is credited with writing so many is an indication of his large contribution. That picture of young George Washington, ax in hand, standing by the cherry tree he had felled, bravely confessing that he had cut it down, is quite ridiculous. To have lied under those circumstances would have been intensely stupid. Why has this story lived? The known integrity of George Washington has kept it alive. Even so, the many poems credited to David indicate that he was a productive poet.

This one-time shepherd was also a man of beautiful modesty. He never swaggered. The nearest he came to it was when he took a census of Israel. Even when he had won his battle against Goliath, he refused to say to those who had sneered at him, "I told you so." Later when it was suggested that he might marry Saul's daughter, he did not take it as a matter of course. He greeted this suggestion with a kind of amazed horror, saying that it was no trifling matter to be the son-in-law of the king.

Being thus modest, thus beautifully humble, he never took the blessings of God as matters of course, He never felt that these blessings had come to him through any merit of his own. His attitude was always, "Who am I, that this gift should come to me?" Thus every gift of God became to him a glad surprise. Every blessing he greeted with eyes sparkling with wonder. He was a man of beautiful humility.

With all this he was naturally a man of irresistible charm. He seems to have had an all but universal appeal—and that is very rare. He cast a spell over gloomy Saul. At first sight he so won the heart of princely Jonathan that this great soul was eager to uncrown himself that he might give the crown to his friend. But the common people loved him, too. "Everything that the king did," says the author, "pleased all the people." He cast a spell over high and low, rich and poor.

For instance, one day he was hiding in a certain cave. With perhaps a touch of homesickness, he said, "How I wish I had a drink out of the old well by the gate of Bethlehem." Three of his soldiers heard him. In spite of the fact that they knew that Bethlehem was in the hands of the enemy, they set out for the well. Hours later they returned, each with a skin of water. With deep gratitude David accepted their gift; but in his sight the water was so tinged by the sweat and blood of sacrifice that it was too sacred to drink. Therefore, he poured it out as an offering to his Lord. Thus he cast a spell over the generation of which he was a part. Not only so, but he has cast a spell over all generations since that far-off day.

What was the crowning characteristic of this shepherd? What was it that bound all these varied gifts into a beautiful whole? It is my conviction that the outstanding characteristic of David was his God-hunger with its resulting God-consciousness. More than any other man in the Old Testament, it seems to me—excepting, of course, his terri-

He Love God
He consulted God
He honored God
His heart was broken when God was displeased

ble fall—he referred the decisions of his life to God. Just as almost everything we do tends to have a self reference, even so, everything that David did seems to have had a God-reference.

When, for instance, he made his first visit to the army of Saul and heard the challenge of Goliath, his heart leaped with excitement and joy. "I have come at a good hour," he said to himself. "I am going to have the privilege of seeing God's champion defeat that boasting pagan." But when nobody volunteered, when he saw in the faces of the soldiers, and even in the face of Saul himself, nothing but fear and shame and defeat, he was at once amazed and deeply grieved.

Then it was that he himself madly offered to fight Goliath. Why? That he might become famous? Not a bit of it! He realized keenly that the cowardice of the soldiers of Israel was a dishonor to God. That he could not endure. No knightly husband was ever more jealous for the honor of his bride than David for the honor of his Lord. It was this that sent him into the battle.

But even then, with all odds against him, how did he dare? Certainly he knew himself no match physically for this giant. It was his sense of God that gave him courage. Saul and his soldiers had their eyes so fixed upon this giant that for them he completely hid the face of God. Naturally, therefore, they were afraid and felt themselves mere pygmies. But to David, with his keen sense of God, it was the giant who became a pygmy to be faced and defeated without fear.

Again, when Saul's faith in David had become fear,

when his love had changed to hate, this one-time favorite was forced to become a hunted outlaw. Everyone doubtless told him "It's your life or his." Then one fateful night, as if arranged by God's own hand, David had Saul completely at his mercy. He might safely have pinned the sleeping king to the earth with his own spear. Not only so, but everybody, friend or foe, would have declared that he had a right so to do.

But this amazing fugitive, to the horror of his friends, passed up his big chance. Why did he do it? He did it because of Saul's peculiar relationship to God. However hard-pressed David might have been, he could not bring himself to stretch forth his hand against the Lord's anointed.

Naturally, by far the blackest period in the life of David was when he was being tortured by remorse for his most ghastly crime. In hot blood he had committed adultery. In cold blood he had committed murder. Of course he had thus wronged the woman in the case, and he had also helped lower the moral tone of his nation. But above all, he had wronged to the death a faithful, loyal subject and friend. How that damning realization must have haunted and tortured him! There is no measuring the agony of that black memory.

But for this shepherd king there was yet a hotter hell even than that! Here is a question from Job (7:20 Moffatt) that David would never have asked:

> If I sin, what harm is that to thee,
> O thou Spy upon mankind?

So keenly conscious was this royal penitent of the harm that he has done God that the torture of it dimmed all other agonies as the sun dims the stars. Therefore, from the flames of this hell he reached trembling hands to clutch at God's skirts and cry:

> Against thee, thee only, have I sinned.
>
> . . . .
>
> Deliver me from bloodguiltiness, O God,
> thou God of my salvation,
> and my tongue will sing aloud of thy deliverance.
>
> —Ps. 51:4, 14

Thus, even in his blackest hour, David put God first.

III

Now what does this story of David have to say to us? I mention only two words:

First, it tells us of our all but infinite capacity to go wrong. "If one had told you ten years ago that you would ever become what you are now, you wouldn't have believed?" I once questioned a pitiful wreck. "If one had told me such a thing," he answered bitterly, "I would have killed him." But no moral attainment, however high, exempts us from temptation. Even Jesus was tempted. Naturally the fact of temptation carries with it the possibility of moral failure. Since all are tempted this word is surely to be taken seriously: "Let him that thinketh he standeth take heed lest he fall" (K.J.V.). That the door to hell always stands open is the verdict of the pagan poet

Virgil. Bunyan also discovered that even hard by the gates of heaven there is a by way to hell.

Here is a word from one who has climbed into higher heights even than this shepherd king. He has been mightily saved. He has tested the validity of his faith through long, stormy years. He has under God made the desert rejoice and blossom as a rose. Yet he has not run past the danger collapse. He writes, "I pommel my body and subdue it, lest after preaching to others I myself should be disqualified." We never climb so high as to be beyond the reach of that grim tragedy.

Secondly, this story also tells us that no fall need be final. In answer to David's penitent prayer God did forgive him. He restored to him the joy of his salvation. Not only so, but he enabled him once more to sing. There may be a bit of truth in the claim that the bird with a broken pinion never soared so high again. But I am sure that it was not true in the case of David. Though every wing seemed broken, once healed by the forgiving touch of God, I think he soared to higher heights than he had ever known before. I feel sure that it was out of a heart throbbing with gratitude and love that he burst spontaneously into the Shepherd's Psalm.

Could I prove that David wrote this psalm? By no means. I could no more prove that he did than you could prove that he did not. But from what we know about him I think this song befits his tuneful lips better than that of any other poet. I love to believe that one day, stirred by hallowed memories and cheered by holy hopes, this greatly forgiven lover burst with birdlike naturalness into this immortal song:

> The Lord is my shepherd; I shall not want.
>
> He maketh me to lie down in green pastures: he leadeth me beside the still waters.
>
> He restoreth my soul: he leadeth me in the paths of righteousness for his name's sake.
>
> Yea, though I walk through the valley of the shadow of death, I will fear no evil: for thou art with me; thy rod and thy staff they comfort me.
>
> Thou preparest a table before me in the presence of mine enemies: thou anointest my head with oil; my cup runneth over.
>
> Surely goodness and mercy shall follow me all the days of my life: and I will dwell in the house of the Lord for ever.
>
> (K.J.V.)

VI. AN AGED PRODIGAL (SOLOMON)

When Solomon was old his wives turned away his heart after other gods.

—I KINGS 11:4

"When Solomon was old." There is a haunting sadness about this phrase that is more depressing than a sob. Here is a tragedy of the twilight: "When Solomon was old." When his step had lost its spring; when his eyes had lost their early sparkle; when the grasshopper had become a burden and he had grown afraid of that which is high—then it happened. At that late hour, made lonely by the fact that many whose hands had once grasped his had passed into the silence—at that time of supreme need, this aged man madly let go the hand of God.

Solomon failed not only at his hour of great need, but also at the hour of his great opportunity. What a witness might have been his! He might have testified with another that of all God had promised in life's morning not one thing had failed. He might have said, "I know from my own experience that the eternal God is our refuge and underneath are the everlasting arms." He might have comforted tempest-tossed souls by saying, "Here is the port into which I put when the storm was on and found it more than sufficient." But instead he gave the lie to all for which he had stood in his yesterdays.

But the supreme sadness of this ugly fall is its finality. It is tragic to see a young chap gather together his all and take his journey into a far country only to waste his substance in loose living. But our grief may be softened by the hope that he is not playing for keeps. Some day he may recover his sanity, return to his waiting father, and make it possible for the festivities to begin in the once-shadowed home. But when an old body heads toward the swine pen, we know that in all probability he will soon reach the point of no return. The climax of this ugly turning away from God is its finality.

I

Look now at Solomon's big chance.

First, he inherited a great position. David had many sons but he chose Solomon as the most fit to wear the crown. Not only was Solomon the choice of David, but we are told that he was the choice of God as well. This is the case in spite of the fact that this gifted king made a bad ending. When Jesus chose Judas to be one of his apostles, he did not choose him because he knew him to be a scoundrel. He chose him just as he chose Peter, James, and John. He chose him as a high adventure of faith. Even so, God chose Solomon for his royal position in spite of his shadowed eventide.

Second, Solomon was greatly blessed, not only because he had a position, but because he had ability to fill that position. A lofty place does not always guarantee a lofty personality or great abilities. "Pygmies will be pygmies still though perched on the Alps." Though I think the wisdom of this man has been greatly exaggerated, he was a man of superb and splendid gifts. I am sure he had abilities equal to his high position. That always means a fine opportunity both for the one who rules and for those who are the recipients of that rule.

Third, Solomon was further enriched by having a consecrated father. David, in Solomon's day, was a very dedicated man in spite of some shady yesterdays. Though he had greatly sinned, he had greatly repented and had been greatly forgiven. Perhaps Solomon had had the privilege of hearing his father sing that song that has gripped the human heart as none other ever written, "The Lord is my shepherd; I shall not want." So truly does this song portray the very heart of God that our Lord took it as a picture of himself, saying, "I am the good shepherd." This high faith David had sought to pass on to his gifted and needy son.

Listen to this father's parting charge. It is full of holy urgency and beauty. "You, Solomon my son, know the God of your father, and serve him with a whole heart and with a willing mind. . . . If you seek him, he will be found by you; but if you forsake him, he will cast you off for ever." Solomon, therefore, had known the enriching power of a good father's life and of a good father's instruction.

Finally, Solomon had had a personal experience of God for himself. Two appearances of God are mentioned; doubtless there were others. First, God came to him in a dream. This fact does not detract from the reality of Solomon's experience. God's message to him is in full character. It is true to the best we know in the Old Testament. He gave this young king the power of choice. He told him to ask any gift at his hands that he chose.

To that invitation Solomon made a satisfying response. He did not ask for things; he did not ask for glory and honor; he asked for an understanding heart. What a beautiful request! In humility he asked that he might have the undergirding of God for the great task set before him. Thus, putting first things first, all these secondary values were to be added unto him. At least this was the case so long as he kept true to his first great choice.

The Lord appeared to him a second time after the building of the temple. He told him graciously that his prayer had been heard. He told him something of his acceptance with him. But he did not leave him without the warning that the dedication he had just voiced must be a continuous dedication. He made it plain that if he failed in this, the great temple that he had built and dedicated would be of no worth at all. Indeed, it would become through his disloyalty and that of his people an utter ruin.

Here, then, are the great assets with which this promising king began his reign. He had high position, vast abilities to fill that position, the undergirding of a good father's life, and above all the undergirding of the everlasting God.

II

What did Solomon do with his big chance? It seems certain that for a time he used his opportunities wisely and well. I am sure that he was an able statesman and a sane and just judge. Not only was he an able ruler, a magnificent monarch, but he was a very shrewd and successful merchant as well. That was all to the good. There is nothing ugly or wicked in making money. Given a right motive, it is just as religious to make money as it is to be a missionary. Of course, that is only true if the money is made by methods that are humanly helpful.

Being a man of peace, he did not squander his wealth in fruitless wars. He did, however waste some of it in military preparations which had no higher purpose, it seems to me, than mere display. Thus, delighting himself in the abundance that was born of peace, he became so prosperous that the author tells us that he made silver as common in Jerusalem as stone.

But if Solomon was wise in the making of money we cannot be quite sure that he was equally wise in the way he made it, nor are we sure that he was wise in the use he made of it. Of course, he used some of it constructively. He became a great builder. One of the most famous temples of all time bore his name. But little of his wealth seems to have been used for the common good. He was foolishly fond of display. He constructed gorgeous palaces for his numerous wives. He gathered about him a pampered court. His drinking vessels were all of pure gold. He acquired money extravagantly and spent it in the same fashion.

But if Solomon was extravagant in the accumulation and squandering of money, he was even more extravagant in the accumulation of wives. He gave himself to a veritable orgy of marrying. Some have suggested that these foreign marriages were at least in part matters of state; that is, Solomon was seeking to avoid war by allying himself with all the rulers of the surrounding nations. He may have thought that it was better to wage private wars in his various palaces than wars that were international. But a more compelling reason, perhaps, for his numerous marriages was his love of display, his desire for the sham glory of possessing the largest and most glamorous harem of any king of his day.

How did this showy king manage with a good conscience to get away with these numerous pagan marriages? Of course he knew that by such conduct he was flouting the law of his God. But were not his motives good? Was he not seeking the high goal of peace? Isn't it right to do evil that good may come? Of course that lie has been exploded a million times, but I doubt that it was ever more ardently believed and practiced than it is today. Many still believe (sometimes in the state, sometimes in the church) that it is right to do evil provided the end in view is good; that somehow we can reach heaven by way of hell. But if everybody who has found that to be false were to say "Amen," it would shake the pillars of the universe.

I think also that Solomon's assurance of his own ability, and especially his high success, had gone to his head. It had given him a sense of superiority to the moral law. Common and stupid folks still had to reap as they sowed. But that was not true of Solomon. He had cunning to manipulate this law and garner wheat from a sowing of weeds.

After speaking to a university congregation some time ago on "The New Birth" a professor took issue. She said that it was not necessary for artists and men of genius to be born anew. Of course, I was not able to argue with her in a convincing fashion. But I could only hint that since these highly gifted souls had to pass through a physical birth in order to get into this visible world, it might be just as necessary for them to pass through a second birth in order to enter the kingdom of God.

The law of gravity operates for a genius just as it does for a moron. But Solomon had become so very successful that he felt himself above the moral law. Therefore he went his gaudy and godless way, feeling himself an exception because of his great gifts and his seeming success.

III

Now what came of this flouting of the will of God? It happened to Solomon as it happens to the most stupid. The man gradually rotted down. As he led one bride after another to the altar he was getting up in years. Some of those brides were doubtless youthful, charming, and clever. They hadn't been in the palace long before they learned that they could flatter this much-married husband. I can imagine they told him he was just as good a man as he was forty years ago. Sad to say, he was silly enough to believe it. This in spite of the fact that his hands shook somewhat, that his face had some ugly furrows, and that his brow had the sparkle of a billiard ball. He persuaded himself that he could deceive the almanac and kick it in the teeth.

We usually face the problem of getting old in one of three ways.

Some simply ignore their birthdays. They shut their eyes.

As a little child sometimes stands in front of us with eyes tightly closed saying, "You can't see me," even so, these confront the calandar. They believe that they can get rid of the passing years by simply ignoring them.

Then there are others who take an even more senseless attitude. They grimly resent the passing of the years. They regard every birthday as a major calamity. They seem as angry at the almanac as they would be at an individual who biffed them in the face when they were not looking. To inquire as to their age is an ugly insult. Thus, growing old resentfully, these take the most direct route to their hated goal. One sure way to get old is to refuse to get old at all.

Then there is a third way; that is, to take it relaxed. I saw a man fall off a horse the other day. He was so deliciously and limberly and relaxedly drunk that he hit the ground just like a wet towel. It didn't hurt him a bit. I wouldn't have minded this fall giving him something to remember it by, but he was so relaxed that he got by without a scratch. If I had fallen off that horse I would have gone down tense and might have broken my bones. The horse called the almanac is going to toss you off some of these days. But take it relaxed, and even if it breaks your bones it will not break your heart. I can imagine that Solomon tried hard to let his wives persuade him that he was just as young as he ever was.

Now as he was young in body, they told him he was even younger in mind. He was not the victim of a closed mind. He was not tied to the narrow religion of his people. He was a liberal. He could wisely see something good in their religion. He not only came to accept the fact that there was something good in every religion, but soon he took the further step of affirming that one religion was as good as another. Then came the final choice. Since one religion was as good as another, why not take the popular faith of his wives? Thus Solomon became so open-minded that paganism came in one door to push faith in God out at another.

As this gifted man rotted down in his inner life, as he became less and less kingly, he became more and more futile and foolish in the management of his kingdom. Milton once said that he who would write a great poem ought himself to be a poem. Certainly he who would render a great service as a king must be kingly in himself. But Solomon, little by little, lost his kingliness. He became less and less effective as a ruler. He became more and more self-centered. He built his kingdom on the underpaid labor and the oppression of his people. Rotting personally, he rotted as a king.

Not only did he thus wreck himself, but he wrecked others as well. He warped his son who was to follow him to the throne. Rehoboam, no doubt, greatly admired his father. He seems to have admired most the way he could oppress people and make them his servants. So when he came to the throne, having chosen as most worthy of imitation that which was worst in his father, he headed at once for disaster.

"Your father made our yoke heavy," his people pleaded. Now therefore lighten . . . his heavy yoke upon us." Listen to his answer: "My little finger is thicker than my father's loins. . . . My father chastised you with whips, but I will chastise you with scorpions." What impression had Solomon made on his son? This impression: The way to live is not to give but to get.

I saw a picture in the paper this week of a father and son, handcuffed to each other. The father couldn't break away from the son; the son couldn't break away from his father. Even so, Rehoboam couldn't break away from his father. Solomon became a wreck, and in so doing he helped to wreck his son.

Not only did he wreck his son, but through his son he wrecked his kingdom. During his own day Solomon's kingdom was showy. The casual viewer would have looked on and said, "What great wealth! What a splendid king Solomon has made." But it was mainly show.

The other day I saw the owner of a beautiful horse approach the beast with a bridle. But he trotted away. When I sought to help by heading the animal, the owner said, "Let him alone. He has a certain disease. He couldn't run fifty yards to save his life."

"Why, then," I said, "he is not worth a thing, is he?" "Not a cent in the world," was the reply. "Well," I questioned, "what do you want with him?" "Oh," he said, "I use him to trade. Two men have each given me ten dollars only this week to take him back after trying him out."

Solomon became a kind of show horse. He was as ugly within as he was showy without. What a tragic failure! And that which brings the tragedy to a climax is that he did so much harm when he might have done so much good. What hotter hell is there than that?

VII. THE HENPECKED KING (AHAB)

There was none who sold himself to do what was evil in the sight of the Lord like Ahab, whom Jezebel his wife incited.

—I KINGS 21:25

Among the kings who had reigned over Israel until this time, there had not been a single one of outstanding worth. All of them had a rather low rating. But it fell to the lot of Ahab to sit at the foot of the class. Jeroboam's record had been very ugly. He had made golden calves for his people that had become a curse. Yet they were intended as symbols of Jehovah. But Ahab so broke with God that he built altars to Baal. Thus he became conspicuously black among a royal flock, not one of whom was white.

The charge against Ahab is that he sold himself. That is, he sold out. This has a very familiar and sinister ring to it. Recently a brilliant young student, an athlete, slipped from a position of high respect to one of contempt over night: He sold out. Even more tragic, an honored minister little more than a year ago stepped from the pulpit to the pit for the same reason. The temptation to sell out in one way or another dogs every man's steps every day. No wonder, therefore, out Lord asks solemnly, "What does it profit a man, if he gains the whole world and loses or forfeits himself?"

I

Though Ahab had sold out, he had not yet become a complete bankrupt. He still had a few white spots on his otherwise shady character. No man is ever wholly bad. Amid the fetid soil of the most depraved soul will often be found some white flower of decency. There were a few qualities possessed by this wicked king that were commendable.

First, he had some sense of fair play. When Elijah returned from his hiding and challenged Ahab to that contest on Mount Carmel, the king accepted. Had Jezebel been in his place I am quite sure that she would not have done so. She would have simply had the prophet arrested and executed. But since she was not there, Ahab showed a finer spirit. No doubt he did this partly because he felt under compulsion. But even at that he was not without this small modicum of decency.

Second, Ahab did not stage any marriage marathon such as was the custom among the kings of that day. Of course, we cannot give him too high a rating for this. I do not think it likely that he, having married Jezebel, was eager for a second venture. Nor do I think that he would have had much choice in the matter, even if he had so desired. Jezebel was not the kind of wife to tolerate a rival. What a difference it would have made for Solomon had he chosen some Jezebel for his first wife. Had such been the case, the other 699 blushing brides he led to the altar would never have cluttered up his palaces. But be the causes what they may, Ahab did not give way to an orgy of marrying.

Third, Ahab was a builder. The author mentions specifically the ivory palace that he built. No doubt it was a thing of such cost and beauty as to be an ornament to the city. I daresay Ahab expected to be remembered by this palace more than by any other achievement. Indeed, such might have been the case but for the fact that the loveliness of this palace served by contrast to emphasize the ugliness of the clay character of its builder.

Fourth, strange as it might seem, Ahab was not without a conscience. True, he did not let that conscience disturb him overmuch. Soon, with the help of his wife, he put it soundly to sleep. But we find that for one brief period he was a bit afraid and ashamed of the evil he had done and of the evil man he had become. Sad to say, his repentance was neither deep nor abiding. But even so, there was a brief moment when God did get through to Ahab in such a fashion as to cause him to look wistfully toward the heights with a feeble longing to climb.

Finally, Ahab was a man of considerable courage. In his last battle, having been fatally wounded, he ordered his charioteer to drive him out of the conflict. But he seems to have rescinded that order. At any rate, he remained in the battle to its tragic end. This he did in spite of the fact that his life blood was slowly flooding the floor of his chariot. Looking at this scene we feel that "nothing in his life became him like the leaving it." Though a moral failure, he still had in him some little good.

II

What was back of this selling out on the part of Ahab? It is the conviction of the author that Ahab's tragedy was born of a bad marriage. If that is true, his story is not unique. Lightly as many of us treat the question of marriage, it is a decision of tremendous importance. In fact almost nothing else will go so far toward determining our laughter or tears, our success or failure, our heaven or hell as the one we marry. This is true of women. I sometimes think it is even more true of men.

Just how Ahab came to make this marriage we are not told. Perhaps as a young prince he met young Jezebel and was captivated by her. Perhaps she cast such a spell over him that he felt life would not be worth living without her. Her name has become a synonym for moral ugliness. Indeed she ranks as the Lady Macbeth of the Bible. She was strong, courageous, dazzlingly brilliant. I am sure also that she could be quite fascinating when she so desired.

Of course her vast superiority over Ahab should have frightened him away. A highly gifted woman is often at a disadvantage in the marriage market. This is the case because she is likely to make her would-be lover feel cheap and inferior. If such is the case, he will almost certainly offer his wares on a market where there is greater demand. Jezebel was doubtless wise enough to put a sparkle in her eyes when Ahab uttered feeble platitudes by way of conversation. Thus she took him in.

In affirming that Jezebel was far superior to Ahab both in intelligence and courage, we do not brand this king as a weakling. It is hard for the tallest anthill to be impressive in the presence of Pikes Peak. And the gamest of dogs would not show up well in a battle with a Bengal tiger. Jezebel had the courage of Lady Macbeth—and more. When this Scottish queen became guilty of murder the "damned spot" that refused to vanish drove her mad. But when Jezebel was facing death she decked herself as for a social function and went to serve as dog meat without a tremor.

I have an idea that however fascinating Ahab found Jezebel that was not his supreme reason for marrying her. She was the daughter of the King of Tyre. Hers was a kingdom that had grown rich through commerce. Ahab saw solid advantages in marrying this brilliant princess. It would help him politically. It might also serve to replenish the none-too-full coffers of his own little nation. But be the reasons what they may, this marriage was Ahab's crowning blunder.

III

Why was this marriage such a failure?

First, these two did not have a common background. They were of different nationalities and of different religious faiths. That is always a barrier. What a tragic number of war marriages between those of different nations ended in failure! Marriages between Roman Catholics and Protestants do not have a high batting average. I think they are never truly successful unless one can wholeheartedly go with the other. Ahab was nominally a worshiper of Jehovah, while Jezebel was a worshiper of Baal.

Besides this, these two differed greatly in their attitude toward their own religion. Ahab, if he cared at all for the faith of his fathers, was entirely lukewarm. Jezebel, on the other hand, was a fiery and fanatical evangelist. She seems to have loved her corrupt and corrupting religion as much as she hated the narrow and strict religion of the Jews. Therefore, she set about driving out the religion of Jehovah with her own religion. This she did with a zeal that would put most professing Christians to shame.

Another reason for the failure of this marriage was that Jezebel henpecked her husband out of all self-respect. A few good women will henpeck their husbands if they can; but having succeeded at the task, they seldom like the finished product. I think no woman is ever happy unless she can look up to her husband for some reason. Of course Jezebel could not have done this with Ahab without getting into a deep cellar. She perhaps loved him in a tigerish fashion, but she could not have respected him.

Perhaps Ahab had some lingering love for Jezebel, but he could not have been happy with her. He knew she held him in contempt. I have an idea that even the courtiers said "Your Majesty" with a smirk.

"George," said a friend, "I thought you were going to the lodge tonight." "I was," came the answer, "but the meeting was postponed." "Why so?" "It had to be postponed because the wife of the Grand Exhalted Invincible Supreme Potentate would not let him out of the house."

Ahab was that supreme potentate. If he possessed a pair

of pants, he never had the privilege of wearing them except in the absence of Jezebel.

IV

Naturally this worked ill both for the king and queen, and for their nation as well. The reign was not really Ahab's; it was Jezebel's. In almost every event you can get a glimpse of her shrewd and powerful hand. Take these three scenes, for instance.

First, when Israel seemed doomed to be taken captive by paganism, Elijah came to the palace. He rebuked the guilty pair, then disappeared for three-and-a-half years while the fields became as parched as the bitter hearts of the queen and king.

As suddenly as Elijah had gone, so suddenly did he return. Then followed the victory on Carmel where God answered by fire. The fickle crowd shouted, "The Lord, he is God; the Lord, he is God." I am quite sure that Ahab joined in this shout. Perhaps he was glad of an excuse to get back to the religion of his childhood.

After such a signal victory he might even have thought that Jezebel would be won over. But when he had reached Jezreel and reported Elijah's victory to Jezebel, we are not told just what she said to him. I am quite sure that only asbestos could have contained her fiery words. Instead of being softened she was hardened. She even sent the gallant prophet flying into the wilderness where he asked for death in the face of what now seemed utter failure. It was Jezebel who turned this signal victory into seeming defeat.

Second, this little domestic scene: Ahab lay on the divan

with his face to the wall. He was in a pout. He refused to eat. Jezebel asked the reason and he poured out the story of the wickedness of Naboth in refusing to sell him his vineyard.

Jezebel glowed. She knew exactly what to do. A little later the wild dogs were feasting off the blood of Naboth by the pool of Samaria. Still later, Ahab took possession of a lovely vineyard. But suddenly the grapes turned sour and the vines withered. The terrified king heard the judgment of Almighty God pronounced against him by his prophet, Elijah.

Too bad! Ahab had felt quite clean. The crime had been that of Jezebel, but now he knew himself not only a murderer, but a cowardly murderer without one redeeming vestige of sportmanship.

Third, the last scene shows Ahab's bid for self-respect. He was going to battle, and he had a visitor, the King of Judah, Jehoshaphat by name, whom he invited to join the campaign.

The King of Judah was willing enough, but being a religious man, he desired to know the mind of God. Ahab was all for that. He knew that Jezebel had prepared the way. He called together a whole mob of prophets. These many prophets were sure of coming victory, and they told the king to go up and prosper. But when Jehoshaphat looked them over he was not convinced.

"Is there not here another prophet of the Lord?" he asked Ahab. That should have been an insult, but it was not. Ahab understood at once. "Certainly there is. But he is a disagreeable chap. There is one—Micaiah—but I hate him because he always prophesies evil against me."

What a revealing sentence! Ahab preferred a liar to one who told the truth, especially if the truth happened to be disagreeable. There have always been those who desire the prophet to voice their convictions rather than his own. Were a prophet to stand in some pulpits today and declare against right race relations, there would be some who would approve. This in spite of the fact that the backward peoples are on the way up all around the world. The shoulders of the Lord God Almighty are behind the movement. To try to stop it would be as futile as to stand in the face of the sunrise and say "Boo" and expect the darkness to settle over the earth again.

Micaiah dared to tell the king the truth—that his adventure would end in disaster. "I told you so," said Ahab. Then in anger he put Micaiah in prison and set out on his campaign telling himself, "I don't believe a word that that old fogey said."

Yet he had misgivings. Thus, half frightened, he disguised himself. In one respect that disguise was a complete success. Not one of his foes found him out. But there was one that did—and that was his sin. For that is one detective that no man ever eludes. "Be sure your sins will find you out."

Look yonder by the pool of Samaria! There are those dogs again. Once more they are having a bloody feast. Yesterday it was the blood of Naboth. Today it is the rich, royal blood of Ahab. "Poetic justice," you say. "It doesn't always happen like that."

"Quite right," I answer. But it always happens in some way. No man ever gets away with anything. "Whatever a man sows, that he will also reap."

"What a tragic ending! It is all the more tragic because it was so needless. Ahab did not have to sell out. Had he only given himself wholeheartedly to his God he would have had victory in himself. Not only so, he might even have won brilliant and dashing Jezebel. Thus a blistering blight might have been changed into a boundless blessing.

VIII. AN ANCIENT MACBETH (HAZAEL)

And Hazael said, "Why does my lord weep?" He answered, "Because I know the evil that you will do."

—II KINGS 8:12

This man Hazael is separated from the Macbeth of Shakespeare by seas and continents and centuries. Yet these two have very much in common. Neither was born to the purple. Both worked their way up from the ranks. Both were once trusted servants of their royal masters. Both received into their hearts the seed of an evil ambition which they allowed to grow. Both ended upon a throne. They each reached the highest position, but they reached that position by descending into the lowest depths. They attained the throne at the price of disloyalty, treachery, and murder. Each killed his royal master with his own hand. I am sure, too, they were alike in this: No nightmarish dream ever suggested to them that they would become the evil men they did.

I

Look at Hazael. He had come from the bedside of King Benhadad, who was very ill. He had been sent by the king to inquire whether his majesty would recover from his illness. When Hazael arrived and put the question to Elisha, he received a ready answer. It was an answer that would have bewildered him very much had he not known what was going on in the deeps of his own soul. The prophet said, "Go, say to him, 'You shall certainly recover'; but the Lord has shown me that he shall certainly die."

Now that was a contradictory statement. How was it that Hazael didn't turn on him in surprise and say, "What do you mean?" The simple answer is this: He already knew. Elisha was saying to him, "Your master would get well, but for you. But you are going to see to it that he does not."

The prophet did not make this announcement in bitterness. He did not make it in anger. He made it in deep grief. According to Moffatt's translation, the prophet's face was filled with horror. According to this translation, that face became wet with tears. With a sob he told Hazael something of what he was going to do because he saw the way he was facing at that time.

At the words of the prophet, Hazael had the grace to blush. He had not yet become a thoroughly bad man. Now, a blush is an index of character. We can judge something of what a person is by what makes him ashamed. Jesus said, "Whoever is ashamed of me and of my words, of him will the Son of man be ashamed." That is not a mere matter of retaliation. Why would Jesus be ashamed of one who is ashamed of him? For the very simple reason that to be ashamed of incarnate Goodness, to blush over the Highest, indicates that the one who blushes is a slave to the lowest. What makes you blush is an indication of what you are.

Hazael blushed at the revelation of the evil in his own heart. That, I repeat, shows that he was not altogether evil. A blush over what is bad is a red flag which conscience waves above the citadel of the soul to show it has not yet fully surrendered to the god of the corrupt. It speaks in favor of Hazael that though he was planning what was treacherous and evil, he still had the grace to turn red with shame.

I think his blush was born of two causes. First, he was ashamed to do the vicious thing that he was planning. He knew it was wrong and he had enough goodness to shrink from it with a kind of horror. Then he was ashamed because he had been detected. He had been caught, in a sense, in the very act. It is a queer freak of human nature that many a man who is not at all ashamed of evil in the deeps of his soul is terribly ashamed to have that evil exposed. Years ago I saw a lovely girl go laughing into the office of the headmaster of her school. Less than five minutes later she came out with a face red with shame and wet with tears. What was the matter? The headmaster had informed her that he knew of her ill conduct. It was not her wrongdoing that made her ashamed, but the fact that she was detected.

Now Hazael did a very natural thing. He told the prophet that he was certainly wrong. He said, in effect, "You are wrong for two reasons. First, I could not do the deeds that you have mentioned because I lack the power. I am only a dog. That is, I lack the ability to accomplish such evil. Furthermore, I am not bad enough. I may be facing in the wrong direction but I can never become so bad that I will actually stain my hands with murder." No man has any idea of how good or how evil he may become. In spite of Hazael's doubts it did turn out just as the prophet had spoken.

Why was this? It was not the fault of the prophet. It is sometimes argued that Jesus, by warning Simon that he was going to deny him made that denial all but a certainty. But that is to misunderstand the situation altogether. Simon did deny Jesus, but not because Jesus had warned him. Rather he did it because he had forgotten that warning. "And Peter remembered," says the story. Then—after the lie had been told, after the denial was an accomplished fact—then he remembered. It was a memory that cured, that led to repentance. But the prophecy of Jesus no more made Peter a denier than the prophecy of Elisha made Hazael a murderer.

As a teacher I have had to say to an utterly careless and indifferent pupil, "You are going to flunk the class if you do not mend your ways." My saying it did not make the pupil fail. The purpose was the very opposite. But it was easy for me to see that he would fail if he did not change. So the prophet said to this gallant officer, "You are headed in the wrong direction and you are going to become a treacherous killer if you keep on the way you are going."

Hazael could not wholly believe it anymore than we can believe the worst about ourselves.

Now this story has to say that which is is of abiding value. First, just as Hazael, we are all on our way to becoming something. We are all changing. I remember years ago seeing a very drab dray, driven by an even drabber driver. This chap was singing lustily as he made his way down the street, "I don't know where I'm going, but I'm on my way." That is a song in which we may all join—at least in part. We are on our way! The anchor's up and we are out at sea. We are on a journey—an eternal journey. We are all going somewhere. This is true of everybody because change is inevitable. We all have to change whether we like it or not.

But there is one thing that is a matter of choice. We can choose the direction of our change. That is fundamental. That is the one thing of supreme importance. The most important fact about you and me is not how far we have climbed toward the heights or how low we have dipped toward the depths. The big question is this: What is our direction? What are we becoming? Remember that we have a whole eternity in which to travel and if we are going wrong in the slightest degree, there is no measuring how far down we may go. If we are going right, there is no measuring how high we may climb.

II

Look at this on its lower level. It is utterly unbelievable how far wrong we can go if we keep traveling in that direction. Let me remind you again that God has set eternity in our hearts. The road on which we travel is an endless road. This is true whether we like it or not. There are some who do not welcome the thought of immortality. There are some who say, "It does not matter to me in the least whether there is an afterlife or not." But that is something over which we have no choice. Always we are going to travel up or down.

I think perhaps the best dog story ever written is Jack London's *Call of the Wild*. How pleasing at first was Buck, that fine Newfoundland dog. But Buck was taken into a new environment, into the wilds of Alaska. Here he became the best husky of the territory. He could pull more than any other dog. But by and by his master became ill and the dog was left too much to himself. He began to wander through the wilds of the forest. One night he heard the howl of a wolf; his bristles went up and he was ready for battle. But he heard it again and again until, when he finally met the wolf, there was no battle. Instead they put their noses together, wagged their tails, sat on their haunches to howl to the distant stars as their ancestors had done thousands of years before. Soon Buck became at home with the wolves. He ended up as leader of the wolf pack, the most vicious of them all. Thus in a few months he had changed from a faithful servant to a wild savage.

If that story is true of a dog, it is even more true of ourselves. Judas is usually taken as a prime example of our capacity to go wrong. Of course, we are largely right in selecting him, though I think I have known many far worse than Judas. He did make a fine start. One day he met a young man who cast a spell over him. Though that young man was a confessed son of poverty and though he laid down conditions of discipleship that must have been hateful to Judas, so tremendous was the spell that this man cast upon him that he forsook all to follow him. Thus Judas became a disciple of Jesus not because the master compelled him—he never compels anybody. He became a disciple of his own choice.

Then later, after a whole night spent in prayer, Jesus chose him with eleven others to be an apostle. Now of course every disciple is not an apostle. These apostles were handpicked. Why did Jesus choose Judas? Not because he was a crook, not because he saw a fatal flaw in him. He chose him just as he chose Peter and James and John—because of what he was and of what he might become. He had a tremendous opportunity. Not only so, but he so met his responsibilities that at the Last Supper when Jesus said, "One of you will betray me," no one turned his eye upon Judas.

Yet in his heart he had gone wrong. He had begun to take money from the treasury; and, reading the pain for his guilt in the eyes of Jesus, the friendship he had once felt had little by little changed to enmity. So startling was that change that there was born a tradition that when Leonardo da Vinci painted "The Last Supper," he used the same model for the Christ that he later used for Judas. Of course it is only a tradition, but it is a startling possibility. It shows how rapid may be our descent if we turn our back on the highest. From right where I now stand and from right where you stand, there stretches a road that goes on endlessly until it loses itself in the quagmires of desolation and death. We have an all but infinite capacity to go wrong.

III

But over against this is the tremendous fact that we have an all but infinite capacity to go right.

One day Jesus met two fishermen. He said to them, "Follow me and I will make you become fishers of men." "I will make you become"—that is an arresting and thrilling word. Our power to become, once our Lord can get our feet turned in the right direction, is beyond measure if we only persist. "In due season we shall reap, if we do not lose heart." This has been demonstrated in countless lives. Who would have dreamed that bloody-handed Saul of Tarsus would end by becoming one of the greatest ambassadors of our Lord? Who would have believed that Mary Magdalene, possessed of seven demons, which means evil at its worst, would have been so transformed in a few months of fellowship with Jesus Christ that she would be the last to leave the cross of crucifixion and first to come in the early dawn of Easter to have her face flooded with the light of the Resurrection?

One told me recently of an ex-moonshiner in the mountains of East Tennessee. A few months ago he was running an illicit still, making some sixty gallons of liquor a day while he himself was one of his own best customers. But a young minister went to him, preached to him the unsearchable riches of Christ; and under the spell of that preaching, he changed the direction of his life. Today he is chairman of the evangelistic committee in his little church.

In giving his humble testimony, he spilled out this unconscious poetry, "I can never be thankful enough to my Lord for his taking the moonshine out of me and filling me with his sunshine." There is no measuring our capacity to go wrong. But thank God, there is no measuring our capacity to go right.

Look how it worked for the apostle John. At our first introduction to him, he was a narrow-minded fanatic. So true is this that he was eager to call down fire from heaven and burn up a little village because it had refused hospitality to his fellow disciples and his Master. This, in spite of the fact that there were many little children and babies in that village. But as he continued to follow Jesus our Lord made him different. When John himself sought to explain that difference he said, "From his fullness have we all received." "That is, I have received of the fullness of his love, the fullness of his life, the fullness of his concern for others. This I have done because I have gone in his direction." Then he added, "This that has begun here is going to go on forever." "Beloved, we are God's children now; it does not yet appear what we shall be, but we know that when he appears we shall be like him, for we shall see him as he is."

There is nothing, I think, that has done more to injure the reputation of heaven than to picture it as a place where we are to sit and wave palms in listless monotony. That would bore one to extinction in a few minutes even here. Heaven is not going to be like that. It is going to be a land of adventure, a land of endless climbing, a land where we shall become more and more like our Lord. This we shall do till, "The very angels of God will look at us and say, 'How like Jesus Christ he is.'" We have an all but infinite capacity to go wrong, but we have an all but infinite capacity to go right.

IV

Since this is true there is but one big question before the house and that is this: What is the direction of your life? What you are is of vast importance. But what you are becoming—that is of infinite importance. So, as we face our amazing possibilities, as we realize that we may dip down forever or may climb upward forever, what is our choice? To help you to face toward the heights, I bring you this winsome invitation from my Lord, "Follow me and I will make you become."

What a charming man was the rich, young ruler. He had everything—courage, decency, honor, a love of life, a love of the heights. But when one day he kneeled in the presence of Jesus and asked how he might get hold of eternal life, Jesus told him, "Go, sell what you possess and give to the poor, . . . and come, follow me," he refused. In spite of so much that was fine we read of him this shocking word: "He went away sorrowful." But Matthew, though a hard-fisted publican took the opposite course. He followed. Thus, one came to the heights, the other missed it. What is your direction?

IX. THE KING WHO FORGOT (JOASH)

King Joash forgot.

—II CHRON. 24:22 (MOFFATT)

I

He forgot. That is a human trait. There are few complaints that we hear oftener than this, "I am so forgetful." Of course, we are aware of the fact that there is a scientific sense in which we never forget anything. But there is a practical sense in which we forget everything. We forget our vows to the church and our vows to each other. We forget our solemn obligations. We even forget God. There is nothing too big, there is nothing too little, for us to forget. Sometimes this forgetfulness may be trifling. It may have a touch of humor about it. It may also have a touch of tragedy and of tears. But there is no trait that is more human than that of forgetfulness.

I am thinking now of two rather able ministers whom I knew years ago. One of them was preaching with great zest and vehemence when he undertook to quote about the most familiar poem in the language: "Sunset and evening star, and one clear call for me!" he shouted. Then he stopped suddenly as if the call had, in reality, come. The listener, however, knew that he had run into the Gibraltar of forgetfulness. Not to be outdone, he started again with greater emphasis, only to run again against that same Gibraltar. Then he shrieked with high enthusiasm, "Oh, beautiful thought." I suppose he himself could smile at it when he got far enough away, but to the listener, while there was a touch of pathos in it, there was also a touch of laughter.

This second minister was a professor in one of our leading universities. He too began a poem almost equally familiar, "I know not what the future has of marvel and surprise." Then he stopped. Quietly he began again, "I know not what the future has of marvel and surprise." "That," he said, "is a familiar poem; doubtless you know it by heart. I do not." Well, he at least retreated with his sidearms. Still there was that about it that made one smile.

Years ago I forgot a wedding. Not only so, it was a church wedding. Not only so, but it was a church wedding for which I had rehearsed. But I completely forgot it. I have not seen a single member of that bridal party since. I do not care to meet them again until I get to where the gates are pearl and the streets are gold. Then I am going to duck behind St. Peter until I see how they take it. Of course, it was inexcusable. It was also ridiculous. I can now manage to smile at it a little, but it has taken many years for me to get that far.

Then there are other times when forgetfulness is sheer tragedy. Here is an extreme case. Some years ago near my home a mother was bending over her washboard one Monday morning doing her washing. Of course she was making quite a noise. By and by, when she looked up from her work, she discovered that her house was in flames. It must have crazed her for a moment, seeing what she did. She dashed into the house and dragged out a few quilts and back again to get a feather bed and some pillows. Then the house reeled and staggered like a drunken man and fell into ruins. Louder than the crash of the falling building was the shriek of the mother as she remembered that her baby was asleep in the house. In her preoccupation or shock she had simply forgotten.

Now whether forgetfulness is serious or tragic, whether it is a matter for laughter or for tears, depends quite largely upon what we forget.

II

What did Joash forget?

There are some things which, if we are wise, we will set ourselves to forget. It is wise, for instance, to forget our failures unless we use them to improve our efforts tomorrow. There are some people who become so occupied with the failures of yesterday that they make a mess of today. By fixing our gaze on our failures, we may become so paralyzed that we no longer make any serious effort at all.

Then it is wise to forget the petty slights and insults that come to us along the way. We all get wounded sometimes. We feel neglected or we fail to receive the appreciation that we are sure we deserve. It is easy when thus hurt to become angry. Sadder still, we often cherish that anger till it hardens into hate and hate tends to harden into hell. Therefore, we should throw away the petty slights and insults and even the real injuries that come to us along the way.

Not only so, but if we are going to be true Christians, having repented of our sins, we are going to forget them also. That is a keen insight that we find in the Old Testament: "I will forgive their iniquity, I will remember their sins no more." That is, God not only forgives our sins, but he forgets them as well. Therefore, what God forgets we have a right to forget.

There are other values we cannot forget except at our vast peril. It was this kind of forgetfulness that worked such fatal consequences for Joash. What, then, did this man forget? He forgot the kindnesses that had been shown him. Oh, you say, "that leaves me out. Nobody ever did me a kindness."

Don't say that. Such an affirmation indicates beyond a doubt that you are not telling the truth. Not only so, but it is all but positive proof that you are a complete grouch. We have all been the recipients of constant kindness both from man and from God. Everything that we hold dear came primarily from God and secondarily through human hands. "What have you," said Paul, "that you did not receive?" The answer to that question is nothing.

This king was no exception. He had been abundantly blessed by kindnesses. When he was a wee baby a vicious woman set herself to destroy every member of his family. His own life was suspended on something more frail than a gossamer thread. But the wife of the priest, Jehoiada, at the risk of her own life, gathered the little mite in her arms and hid him. Then through the coming days she, with her husband, became in a sense father and mother to him. They trained him in the religion of his fathers. At a tender age they put him on the throne. As a result of their kindness be became a religious man, and for a time a genuinely useful king.

It was Joash who set himself under the inspiration of the teaching of the priest Jehoiada to the repairing of the temple. He raised money through the chest of Joash that is famous to this day. Under this king's leadership there came what amounted to a revival of religion among his people. Thus he had not only been greatly blessed by his teacher, but he had the yet greater privilege of becoming a blessing to his people. Countless blessings had come to him from the hand of God and from human hands, just as to you and me. But this king made the tragic blunder of forgetting all the beautiful. He remembered only the ugly and unpleasant.

III

Why did he forget?

Now there is a sense in which memory seems a capricious and arbitrary creature. One seldom knows what he is going to remember and what he is going to forget. But memory is still subject in great measure to control. We have considerable choice of what we forget and what we remember. We are urged over and over throughout the word of God to remember certain things. "Remember also your Creator in the days of your youth." "Remember all the way which the Lord your God has led you." Jesus said as he was going away, "Do this in remembrance of me."

Why are we so forgetful? Sometimes we forget because we are preoccupied. Our minds are crowded with something else. When I forgot that wedding it was not because I was indifferent to the lovely couple seeking my services. They both belonged to my church. The young man had been converted under my ministry. (I am afraid he may have backslid under it, too.) But something happened that day that was out of the ordinary. Something happened that took up my time and attention so that it simply crowded out the thought of the coming wedding. I forgot because I was preoccupied.

There are other times when through sheer conceit we take the kindnesses that come to us as matters of course. I am quite sure that this, in part, was the case with Joash. He had been shown every consideration but he said, "Why not? Am I not a king? Am I not born to the purple? Of course these people seek to please me! Of course they seek to help me! Of course God's mercies rest upon me! Look at who I am! It is nothing more than I deserve." There is no greater help toward forgetting God's mercies and ending in ingratitude than sheer conceit.

Perhaps the big reason Joash forgot was that he wanted to forget. There are times when remembering is an annoyance. Some years ago a young chap came to see me to "make a touch." I listened to his story and he had a good one. But I had seen him in conversation with a friend just before he came to me and so I excused myself. The friend was close by. I sought him and asked, "Do you know the man who has just been talking to me?" "Yes," was the answer. "Did he ever borrow any money from you?" "Yes," he replied. "Did he pay you back?" "No," was the answer. Then I returned to my man with this question. "Do you know this man to whom I have just been speaking?" "Yes," he said. "Did you ever borrow money from him?" "Yes," was the answer. "Did you pay him back?" At that he popped his fingers in wide-eyed amazement and said, "You know, I forgot that." He doubtless forgot it because he wanted to forget.

After the death of Jehoiada Joash, influenced by his nobles, turned from the religion of his people to become an idolater. The prophets rebuked him. Among those who sought earnestly to call him back to the faith of his youth was the son of Jehoiada, Zacharias. Instead of listening to him, however, the king became angry, not at the disease but at the physician. Suffering from wounded pride he refused to remember the kindness of Jehoiada and the kindness of Jehoiada's son. He forgot their kindnesses because he chose to let that memory be crowded out by something ugly, a desire for revenge.

Now as it is possible to crowd out the beautiful with the ugly, so we can crowd out the ugly with the beautiful. Years ago George R. Stuart, a saint of princely gifts, came to preach for me in Washington. He was a magnificent mountaineer. Indeed, he was so grandly homely that it was a genuine asset. When I went to the train to meet him, I saw that he had acquired an additional touch. Two of his upper front teeth were missing. From mere homeliness he had thus attained ghastliness. I looked at him with a kind of horrified amazement and wondered how he was going to get by with a handicap like that.

When I presented him to my congregation he walked boldly forward, patted himself on the shoulder, and said, "Two or three months ago I took to hurting in this shoulder. I went to see the doctor and he said, 'It's your teeth.' I said, 'It's no such thing; they don't reach down that far.' But I had to have them out and my doctor made me a beautiful plate. But just before I started up here, I broke my beautiful plate. My wife didn't want me to come, but I said, 'Thank the Lord, I still have my tongue left. When I get up there, I'll explain it to the people. The sensible folks will understand and it doesn't make any difference about the fools nohow.' Now, I am here with my tongue. If any of you are not interested in my tongue, you can just look at the hole."

Thus that man took a liability and changed it into an asset. Even so, this man Joash took a great asset, the ministries of a faithful father and of a faithful son who in loyalty to God had supported him and had rebuked him when he needed rebuking, and turned what was gold into something far worse than mud. He crowded out the best with the worst.

IV

Now what came of it all? What was the result of his forgetfulness? How did it all end? Through this forgetting of the kindnesses he became an ingrate. "Think" and "thank" both look and sound amazingly alike. And in a sense they are related. The reason we don't thank more is because we don't think more. Forgetting the kindnesses, failing to think of the tender ministries that had protected his childhood, that had guided his youthful steps, that had given him strength and courage for his mature years, forgetting all this, he had no sense of gratitude. He became an ingrate.

Now ingratitude is a very respectable and common sin, but it is just as cruel as it is common. The greatest of all the poets calls it a fiend. It is not simply an ordinary fiend —it's a marble-hearted fiend. It is about the most cruel of all sins. Sometimes it is aggressively cruel as it was in the case of Joash. He inflicted bodily harm on the man who had rebuked him. He became guilty of cold-blooded murder because he had given away to the ghastly sin of ingratitude.

But ingratitude, perhaps, does its most deadly work not aggressively but passively. It is in our failure to express the appreciation that is really in our hearts that we are guilty of some of our most cruel sins. What a pity it is that we do not have the thoughtfulness and the gratitude to say in the here and now to those with whom we live and with whom we are bound up in a bundle of life what we are going to say about them when they are no longer here. It has been my lot to hold a great many funerals. But by far the saddest funerals I have had to hold were the ones where I knew that somebody was trying to say to the dead what he was so sorry he had failed to say to the living.

Through his ingratitude Joash cheated himself. He robbed himself of one of life's finest treasures. This is true because whatever wealth may come into your hands, if with this treasure there is no gratitude you are still a poverty-stricken wretch. Further, he robbed himself of one of the best and finest ways of helping others. This is true because everybody needs appreciation. To refuse to give it is to cruelly cheat our fellows. Therefore, in taking the course of forgetfulness and becoming an ingrate, Joash cheated himself. He cheated his fellows. He cheated God. So low did he sink that his own people murdered him while he lay in bed, desperately wounded. When they buried him, it was not among the kings. So unkingly had he become that they would not let him rest among his royal ancestors. He lost everything because he forgot and in forgetting became an ingrate.

So what? We are to go right where he went wrong. We need to sing every morning as we wake:

> Bless the Lord, O my soul: and all that is within me, bless his holy name.
>
> Bless the Lord, O my soul, and forget not all his benefits:
>
> Who forgiveth all thine iniquities; who healeth all thy diseases;
>
> Who redeemeth thy life from destruction; who crowneth thee with lovingkindness and tender mercies;
>
> Who satisfieth thy mouth with good things; so that thy youth is renewed like the eagle's.
>
> —Ps. 103:1-5 (K.J.V.)

The only way to drive out the forgetfulness that blights and damns is by remembering those mercies that uplift and save the soul.

X. A ROYAL RUIN (UZZIAH)

That ruined him.

—II CHRON. 26:16 (MOFFATT)

Here is a brief bit of biography written from God's viewpoint. A friend told of seeing on the bottom of a capsized vessel in the Columbia River this advertisement in loud capitals, "I DRINK HILL AND HILL." A little later, again passing that way, he saw how some wise unknown had finished the sentence in equally loud capitals, "AND I AM A WRECK." Here, too, is a wreck. It is the most tragic of all wrecks—that of human personality. "That ruined him," declares this author as he looks upon one who had so much and made so little of it.

I

Who was this man?

This is the story of Uzziah. He had a second name, Azariah. Both names carry a strong religious flavor—"Jehovah my strength" and "Jehovah my help." He was a brilliant and able king. He was kingly not only in position but in his wise handling of his responsibilities. He came to the throne when he was little more than a lad. (He was only sixteen.) Yet he seems from the beginning to have played the part of a man. He reigned over his people for fifty-two years. That is the longest reign that any Jewish king ever enjoyed except Manasseh.

Uzziah was interested in all the interests of his kingdom. He was a builder. The first assertion made of him is that he built Eloth. He also built towns in the territories that he had taken from certain surrounding tribes. He strengthened the walls of his own city. He used the shrewdest engineers of his day to contrive machines upon these walls for the hurling of large stones and arrows. He worked constructively.

Naturally, being a citizen of his age, he was a military man. He kept an excellent standing army. He equipped his soldiers with the best equipment of his day. With this well-trained and well-equipped army, he warred victoriously. He did not allow his little nation to become the stomping ground for the armies of the nations round about.

Then, too, he was interested in stock raising and in agriculture. He was wise enough to give attention to the real source of all wealth—the land. He was in a sense a royal farmer.

I shall never cease to be grateful that it was my privilege to be raised on a farm. Though I have been exposed to some of our best schools, few lessons from them have been of greater value than those I learned on the farm. One important lesson I learned was this—I don't like farming!

Now, since Uzziah was wisely interested in all the

interests of his people, his nation was prosperous. Not only so, but he made his kingdom to be respected far and wide. In fact, he gave it a standing such as it had not known since the days of showy Solomon. "He was marvelously helped, till he was strong."

Being thus highly successful, he gained a secure place in the hearts of his people. He became a national hero. This was true not only for the groundlings but also for the best minds of his nation. This was especially true of a certain brilliant young aristocrat named Isaiah. It speaks well for this king that even after tragedy struck, Isaiah held him in such honor as to become his biographer (II Chron. 26:22).

So much did youthful Isaiah honor and trust King Uzziah, that when he passed from the palace to a pesthouse, then from that pesthouse to the cemetery, it left for him the loneliest possible place against the sky. When this honored king had gone, it was for Isaiah almost as if God had gone. Indeed, it was as he looked past the vacant throne of his honored and loved hero that he became able to see the throne that was not vacant. He saw the Lord high and lifted up.

This tragic passing of Uzziah was used of God to bring Isaiah into a new day. Having taken his eyes off a king, he saw the King. This vision of God did not make this possible prophet shout for joy. It rather broke his heart. It drove him to cry in bitterness of soul, "Woe is me! For I am lost; for I am a man of unclean lips, and I dwell in the midst of a people of unclean lips."

Having thus confessed, his sorrow was changed into joy. This was the case because his lips were at once touched by a live coal from God's altar. Then he heard that voice that still speaks to every repenting soul: "Your guilt is taken away, and your sin forgiven."

Having come thus to see God and to see himself, he came next to see his mission. He heard this divine voice saying, "Whom shall I send, and who will go for us?" There is no compulsion back of the response of Isaiah. He was not a conscript. He was a volunteer. "Then I said, 'Here I am! Send me.'" Having thus given himself to God, God accepted him and used him and made him a mighty prophet. He made him also a statesman who exercised greater political power perhaps than any other man since King David. But even this remaking of Isaiah did not change Uzziah's defeat into victory. He ended a moral failure.

II

What wrecked this king? Where was dropped the spark that reduced this palatial personality to charred ruins? Where began the leak within the vessel that set the waters of desolation and death to roaring above this sunken ship? On the surface it would seem that the fatal sin of Uzziah was that he presumed to take upon himself the office of the priesthood. His was not the role of a priest. When, therefore, he thus presumed, the priests, led by Azariah, made a strong protest. That protest so angered the king that his face became scarlet with rage. It was against this scarlet background that these priests discovered the glaring whiteness of leprosy.

But it was not the mere effort of this king to play the part of priest that brought about his ruin. That was only a symptom. The real evil, the eating cancer that destroyed Uzziah, was just this—he had run past God! "He was marvelously helped, till he was strong." Having arrived, however, he decided he did not need God anymore. Thus this wise and able king became a victim of his own success. As sometimes happens to a bee, he was drowned in his own honey.

Now the fact that he allowed his success to become his ruin does not mean that success in itself is wrong. Success is no more a sin than failure is a virtue. It is our right and our duty to succeed if we can, just as it is an ugly sin to fail if we do so through our own indifference and laziness.

Uzziah's success became a sin because it led to pride and self-sufficiency. Of course, this is not always the case. Success may be a roadway to deepest humility. That is always true if we regard it aright. Success no more has pride as its inevitable goal than failure has humility as its inevitable goal. Some of the most humble people I have ever known have been highly successful. Even so, some of the most conceited swaggerers I have known have been the dullest of failures.

In this latter group I would place one man whom I have known for long years. He is not a bad man; he is rather a kindly bore. Trained for his chosen profession, he has been a consistent failure in that profession. But this failure seems to have made him only the more cocksure. Thus, he is not only an authority in his own field, but in every other. To encounter him in the social circle is to make any effort at conversation unnecessary. All anyone is called upon to do is to nod agreement.

Just as a superb failure may be full of swagger, so the most successful may be beautifully humble. Billy Graham has occupied the limelight for the last decade to a degree greater perhaps than that of any other preacher who ever lived. He has drawn by far the largest crowds. He has had the greatest response. He has met with applause and approval from the learned and the unlearned. Yet a friend—not a member of his staff—writing of him recently, said, "He is the most humble man I have ever met."

Yet success is a heady wine. This is the case because it has a great tendency to make us self-sufficient. Having succeeded, we are prone to give all the credit to ourselves. That was the folly of the rich farmer. He had had abundant crops. His barns were filled to overflowing. But he had nobody to thank for it but himself. He forgot the men who helped to make his success possible. He forgot God, who had given him his life and all else. Therefore, he was called a fool, not because he succeeded, but because he allowed his success so to minister to his pride as to shut both man and God out of his heart.

III

"That ruined him." We can now understand the "that" of which the author is speaking. Uzziah was not ruined by his success; he was ruined by being so spiritually blind and stupid as to take all the credit to himself. No man has a right to do that, be he king or peasant. "What have you," questions Paul, "that you did not receive?" The only adequate answer to that question is "Nothing." Everything that is of worth came to us fundamentally as a gift.

To build life on the foundation of our own self-sufficiency is to build upon a lie. It is to ignore the facts of life and that spells disaster. This is the case when we ignore the physical facts. The man who presumes to live without eating will die. The man who presumes on the law of gravity will be crushed. The man who presumes on fire will be burned to a cinder.

If to ignore the physical facts of life spells disaster, how much more sure will be that disaster if we ignore the supreme fact, the fact of God? Yet there are few sins to which we are more prone. We ignore God in order to get to play that role ourselves. This temptation has dogged humanity from the beginning. "You will be like God," said the tempter in the old Genesis story. We have always wanted to play God. We have always desired independence, absolute freedom, the capacity to do as we please. But such an attitude has never worked.

We are trying it now in a big way among the nations. The primal command was this: "Have dominion." How marvelously we have carried out that command in the realm of the visible! As did Alexander the Great, we feel we have conquered our little world. We are soon to become masters of outer space. But in spite of this, we have not found peace. By thus increasing our powers of destruction, we have only added to our torturing fears. Said a certain Russian, "The universe has passed under new management." But that new management is causing us to hang over hell every morning.

This temptation to get on without God also constantly dogs the church. Individual churches often grow and become powerful only to die of their own self-sufficiency. Here is one such. So sure is it of itself that it passed the following resolution: "Whereas we are rich and increased in goods, be it resolved that we announce to all and sundry that we have need of nothing." Yet "nothing" was all this church did possess. This was the case because the living Christ was even then having to stand and knock at the door of this highly successful church.

This pride, this self-sufficiency also threatens every individual. How easy it is to blame circumstances or to blame our fellows for our failures. How easily also do we take sole credit for our successes, for the blessings that have come to us through others and through the good grace of God. That always spells disaster.

What a true story is that of the frog who decided to spend the winter in the deep south! Having no conveyance of his own, he decided to "thumb" his way to that land of summer. At once he put his resolution into effect with the result that soon two wild geese who were passing overhead, saw him and were kind enough to respond to his call.

But having come from the heights to aid this lowly chap, they were at a loss as to how to go about it. But the wise frog, having thought things through, had a plan. He produced a good string, and gave one end of the string into the beak of *A* and the other in that of *B*. Then with firm jaws, he took hold of the middle. At once this ingenious flight began.

So unique was the adventure that all the birds looked on with high admiration. Not only so, but when a farmer looked up from his task to see this strange sight, he too was filled with both amazement and admiration. "Who invented that?" he shouted. Then the frog, with no thought of how impossible the flight would have been without his friends, felt he could not possibly miss this opportunity to boast of his greatness, answered, "I invented that." An instant later a handful of minced frog was lying at the farmer's feet saying, "Pride goes before destruction, and a haughty spirit before a fall."

The way of pride and self-sufficiency is always, I repeat, a sure road to disaster. Whether we confess it or not, we always are utterly dependent upon God. "I am the vine, you are the branches." What relation does the branch have to the vine? It is one of constant contact and of constant receiving. But above all else, it is one of utter and absolute dependence. For the branch, to assert its independence is not to become green and fruitful. It is surely to wither and die.

This passing of Uzziah from a palace to a pesthouse was, therefore, not inevitable. It came of his independence toward God. It was born of his own self-sufficiency. I am quite sure he desired the favor and friendship of God. But as so many others, he desired it upon his own terms. Everybody would like a warm, rich, radiant, religious experience, if he could have it on his own terms. Every student in school would like to make 100 on every recitation, if he could do so on his own terms. But that is impossible. Before God can depend on us, we must depend on him.

Now, how long are you going to be without the power of God in your life? Just so long as you are willing to be without it. You may deeply desire God's help. You may even ask for it. But if you ask with it in the back of your mind that if he fails to help you can muddle through some way, then you will be left to muddle through. It is only when our desperate needs make us willing to give all, that we are capable of receiving God's all. No victorious help is possible for one who is independent toward God. No ultimate defeat is possible for him who depends on God. "He who believes in him will never be disappointed." (Moffatt.)

XI. A ROYAL MODERNIST (HEZEKIAH)

He broke in pieces the bronze serpent that Moses had made.

—II KINGS 18:4

In calling Hezekiah a modernist I have no reference to that rather threadbare controversy between fundamentalist and modernist. I am only saying that this youthful king did a bit of thinking for his own day. Thus thinking, he dared to smash to bits the bronze serpent that Moses had made, calling it only a piece of brass. Such a shocking deed required either great rashness with a mixture of stupidity or genuine insight backed by high courage.

The latter was the case, because that serpent had gathered to itself a sacredness born of long centuries of veneration. It had upon it the very finger marks of their great leader, Moses. Not only so, but less clearly seen, there were also upon it the finger marks of God. In a distant and desperate day it had been of great service. So wonderfully had it played its part that Jesus made use of it in speaking of his own mission: "As Moses lifted up the serpent in the wilderness, even so must the Son of man be lifted up." Yet this young king knew nothing better to do with this honored object than to smash it to bits.

I

How, I wonder, did his people react? I imagine that it divided them into at least three groups.

There were no doubt those who looked upon change as a bit of an end in itself. These of course burst into loud applause. "That," they asserted with enthusiasm, "should have been done long ago. With that roadblock out of the way we can now make some real progress." There are always with us those who, as the ancient Athenians, like to spend their time in hearing and telling some new thing. To them change means progress, regardless of the nature of the change.

Sometimes these people, with their passion for change, get into the pulpit. No sooner do they reach a new pastorate than they hasten to change everything in sight. Their predecessors have left nothing of worth. They look upon all that came from yesterday with a kind of contempt, whether it be a custom, a faith, or a person. Often they seem more concerned about the new than about the true.

I knew one such person years ago. He was a highly cultured man with many fine qualities. But so far as I remember he never once took a text in which he believed. He would first bleed it white. Then, when he sought to give it a blood transfusion out of his own brain, I often felt that the effort weakened him without giving strength to the congregation. Such negative preaching, however new, is not likely to change a valley of bones such as that of Ezekiel into a parade ground for an exceeding great host. It is more likely to reduce such a host to shattered bones.

Sometimes, though perhaps less often, the apostle of change is in the pew. He is eager to overhaul the whole organization of the church. All officers should be put out and new ones brought in. Then, above all, the minister must be remade. If he is too stubborn to learn wisdom, then he must move. There are for such people only two really good ministers, the one who served yesterday and the one they are expecting tomorrow. "We want a new minister," said one such man. "We should like one who is religious if we can find him. If not, we want one that is religiously inclined. But come what may, we must have a change."

The stand-patters were also present when this king did his rash deed. Some were saddened by it. They felt that they had been robbed, that something beautiful had been destroyed. Others were angered. They vowed they would attend church no more. Certainly they would make no further contribution. These hated all change. Rip Van Winkle was their ideal saint, save that he slept in the open instead of in church. Their favorite forest was not such as changed from the Easter beauty of spring to the golden glory of autumn. It was one that was petrified and changed not at all.

In almost every church there are at least a few who regard the new as they would a suspected person in enemy country. Their best reason for taking any action is that they have always done it that way. Any new translation of the Bible fills them with horror, not because it is faulty or misleading, but because it is different. Indeed, it often seems difficult to move so much as a chair in some churches without setting it down on the sore toe of some saint. Such people are by nature and practice the foes of all change.

Some years ago a zealous young minister became pastor of a church that had sought to "hold its own" for almost a century. He came to his new charge from halfway across the continent. Therefore, he knew very little of the staid congregation he was to serve. The very first Sunday, instead of indulging in target practice, he shot to kill. The result was that when he gave the invitation at the close of the service more than a dozen people came forward.

That was something different. Some became so excited over it, as the young pastor continued such practice, that they told their friends. These friends told others, until soon the church was filled to standing room at every service. Of course many rejoiced. One lovely old official said to his new minister: "I'm so glad you made this change before we had time to tell you that it couldn't be done."

But that favorable verdict was not universal. One day a sweet old spinster said to her pastor with real sadness, flavored by a touch of anger, "Before you came we old members could come to church and sit anywhere we pleased, even if we were late. Now, if we are not ahead of time, we often have to stand." Such a thrilling situation, it seems to me should have resulted in glad hallelujahs. But for her it was only ground for groans.

Then there were those who viewed this serpent smashing not simply with their emotions, but with intelligent eyes.

Thus seeing, they approved, not simply because they loved change for its own sake, but because they thought this change helpful. That is the real test of the right or wrong of any change. If it is humanly hurtful, it is likely to be wrong. If it is humanly helpful, it is likely right.

Why did Hezekiah smash this serpent? It was not to shock the people. There are still those of the adolescent type who believe in the shock treatment. Indeed, this is sometimes good, but it was not the purpose of this young king. No more was he seeking to win applause. Nor was he seeking to discredit the serpent by denying that it was the work of Moses. Least of all did he turn wrecker because the serpent had never been of any value. He was not denying that many, by God's grace, had been healed by it.

Why then, I repeat, did he break it? This was one reason: The evil that it had been made to cure no longer existed. The people of Hezekiah's day had problems, but fiery serpents were not one of them. There is no sense in keeping a remedy for a disease that no longer exists. There is no use in building factories to manufacture covered wagons when nobody travels in that fashion anymore.

Not only had this revered object ceased to be of use; it had become a hindrance. Some had made it into an idol. Thus they had made into an end something that at best had been only a means. Intended to turn the eyes and hearts of the people toward God, it was now turning them in the opposite direction. Therefore, this earnest young king decided to brave the wrath of many by smashing it to bits. "Here," he said, "is something that needs to be changed; hence, I am going to change it."

II

This is of interest to us because we also have to do with change. There are always idols being smashed for us or idols that we smash ourselves. All changes are not of the same kind. There are some about which we have little or no choice. There are others that we make of our own free will.

For instance, our world is constantly changing and there seems little we can do about it. A certain psalmist was confronted by that problem long ago:

> The pillars of the State are falling:
> what can a just man do?
> —Ps. 11:3 (MOFFATT)

Nothing is one answer. Run is another; "Flee like a bird." But this did not satisfy the poet's conscience. He was convinced that however hopeless his situation he could still vote on the right side, could still stand in his place and be true.

There are changes beyond our control that we must accept and to which we must adjust. A devoted young family is surely a thing of joy and beauty. But, like it or not, that family changes. The children grow up. Of course, parents accept that with gladness—that is, they are glad for them to grow physically—but some resist their growing emotionally. They wish to keep them as dependent as babies. I am thinking of an intelligent man of fifty who is as incapable of making a choice as a small child. For far too long all his choices were made for him.

Here and there is a mother who is eager to hold first place in the heart of her son even after he has a family of his own. This is what has made some mothers-in-law the high explosive for many a home. Blessed is the in-law who can gladly take second place. That old idol of first place must be smashed, or the marriage is likely to end in tragedy.

There is another idol we must break, or else be broken by it. That is youth. Like it or not, all of us change. We pass from youth to middle life; from middle life to old age. Some resent this. They are more afraid of the almanac than of the atomic bomb.

Years ago, when I was just turning forty, I went to see a friend of sixty-nine. This man was one of the superb preachers of that day. In spite of the wide span of years that separated us, he took a fatherly interest in me and I honored him greatly.

Suddenly in the course of our conversation he turned to me and said with utter desperation: "It's awful! It's awful for one who has lived his life in the thick of things as I have to get old and get where he can't do it anymore."

I was startled and saddened. I even felt that he had let me down. When, a few minutes later, I was alone I had the first conversation with myself about getting old that I had ever had.

"Look here," I said, "that is coming to you one of these days. When it comes I want you to meet it more gallantly than that. You haven't done much, but you have done more than anybody ever thought you would do, including yourself. Now when you strike out, don't throw down your bat in a huff. Try to say to the oncoming batter 'I have not knocked as many home runs as I'd have liked, but thank God, I've had the privilege of playing the game.'"

From there I began to prepare myself for the breaking of the idol of youth. So far, I have met this change joyfully. Strange as it may seem, I am content to be old. I have no desire to be young. I have fished that stream out and am now fishing in more placid, yet equally joyous, waters.

There are also changes that are matters of choice. Perhaps you are convinced, for instance, that your church is not as it should be. If such is the case then, being a part of it, you can help to change it.

In a certain church that seemed on the point of becoming a mausoleum a group of young parents decided to do something about it. They felt that some of the fault might lie with their pastor. Then came the real test. "What is wrong with *us?*" they questioned. They began with one simple answer. "At the evening services we have been expecting our pastor to kindle a fire with one or two sticks of wood. Suppose we help him by being there."

I don't know how the experiment will work out, but I am sure of this: If they prayerfully follow through, it will bring a new springtime to their own hearts and to their church.

There are changes that you as an individual can choose for yourself. Jesus tells of a certain chap who looked at himself one day and did not like what he saw. "I am in a mess," he confessed. "I am dying of hunger in spite of the fact that even the hired servants of my father have bread

Your opinion helps us improve our service to you. Will you criticize this book for us, please?

LIVING WITH ROYALTY

Where did you first hear about this book or see it advertised?

Clergy ☐ ?   Church Member ☐ ?   Not a Church Member ☐ ?

enough and to spare. I don't have to continue as I am. I can still find a place at the feast of the fullness of life. But if I find that place I am the one that has to decide." And decide he did—"And he arose and came to his father."

III

Perhaps there is one fault to find with the rash conduct of this king. For the present at least he put his chief accent on the negative. He sought to destroy evil by a frontal attack. He smashed the serpent, but we are not told what he did to fill the vacuum. If he did not lead these one-time worshipers of the serpent to a higher worship we may be sure that their conversion was not lasting.

"Do not resist one who is evil," said Jesus. What a queer word from one who resisted evil more effectively than any other who ever lived, and resisted it unto death! But what our Lord is urging is not an easy tolerance of evil, but a different tactic of fighting it. He does not approve of the frontal attack.

This is the case because he knew that by such method whatever victory we win will likely be temporary. The unclean spirit, though once driven out, found it easy to return because the house from which he had been driven was empty. Even were the destruction of evil permanent it would guarantee no positive good. Why pull up the tares if the wheat is destroyed by the same process? The result would not be a field of golden grain but a barren waste. The only real enemy of evil is good. The only conqueror of darkness is light. It was not by smashing false gods that the primitive Christian changed that hard Roman world. It was by holding up Jesus Christ.

The village school building of my boyhood stood in a forest of scrubby oaks. When autumn came and all the trees decked themselves in scarlet and gold, these hardy oaks joined the colorful parade. But when the wintry winds came with their rain, sleet, and snow and called for an offering of leaves to fertilize the earth; when the other trees gave their very all, these oaks were as miserly as mummies. They seemed unwilling to spare a single leaf.

But by and by the winter with her strong blasts would give up, either from discouragement or disgust. Then the days would grow a bit longer and warmer. At last an unseen power would climb through the trunks of those tough trees out to the very end of the smallest twig. Then a mighty but silent voice would say to each brown stubborn leaf—"Move over." And what the howling winter, with all its power, could not do, spring did by the giving of new life. "This I say then, Walk in the Spirit, and ye shall not fulfil the lust of the flesh." (Gal. 5:16 K.J.V.)

XII. A GOD-GIRDED PAGAN (CYRUS)

I gird you, though you do not know me.
—ISA. 45:5

Cyrus is one of the giants of all history. He was a great conqueror. God opened doors before him and mighty nations dropped like overripe fruit into his hands. Not only was he a conqueror, but he was also a wise and gracious ruler. In fact, to the keen and understanding Greeks, he was an ideal king. Though they themselves had had some great rulers, yet in spite of their patriotism, they gave the highest rating to this foreigner. To them he represented kingliness at its best.

What is still more impressive, however, is that not only did the Greeks regard Cyrus highly, but he was held in little less honor by the narrow-minded and puritanical Jews. They were glad to accept him as their deliverer. They were glad to claim him as the one chosen of God to break their yoke and to bring them back to the land of their fathers. Thus he was honored both by Gentiles and Jews, by those who worshipped many gods and by those who worshipped only one God. We may therefore take seriously the word that God spoke through his prophet, "I gird you, though you do not know me."

I

Now the fact that God girded this pagan, if a bit of a shock, is also heartening. It gives this assurance:

> The love of God is broader
> Than the measure of man's mind,
> And the heart of the Eternal
> Is most wonderfully kind.

That is, God loves not only believers, but also those who do not believe. It makes us sure that there is a light that enlightens every man; that in every man, in every church, even in every religion there is some good. Our missionaries have learned that they are not to begin their work among those whom they seek to help by tearing to bits all on which they have built in the past. They are rather to take what is true and seek to build upon that. No people, nobody has been left without some bit of witness.

Now since God girded this pagan, we can believe that he girds every man. Paul, in his letter to the Colossians, said, "All things were created through him and for him." That is, God has a purpose and a plan for every life. Horace Bushnell has a great sermon on this text entitled, "Every Man's Life a Plan of God." I was not able to find and read that sermon; therefore this of mine may be the poorer for that lack.

"Every Man's Life a Plan of God"—All that this great

preacher meant by that I cannot say. I do not take him to mean that we are all just as God intended us to be. Though God plans every life we do not all carry out that plan. God is the architect; we are the builders. Our supreme tragedy is that we too often refuse to build according to his plan.

When I was pastor in Washington, I sometimes met on my walks a man who looked little better than a nightmare. Yet I knew that when that man first came from his native state he was a magnificent figure. He had been elected more than once to the United States Senate, but he had fallen into the destroying grip of alcohol. Thus that once-fine body had been blighted and that fascinating personality had been torn into shreds and tatters. Therefore for one to affirm that this shambling wreck was a part of a divine plan would be an ugly slander against God. God does have a plan for every life, even for pagans, but all do not build according to his plan.

II

This universal girding of God explains in some measure the good that we find among the unorthodox. Of course, that good is often exaggerated. It is fashionable today for the writer of fiction to picture the renegade of the community as the one who in times of crisis shows the most compassion. Sometimes that may be the case. It certainly is not the rule, however. Other things being equal, what a man believes really does color his conduct. Therefore, when one affirms, "The best people I have known have not belonged to any church," I have, in sober honesty, to say that such has not been my experience. Far the best I have known have belonged to the church. Yet this is not to deny that I have known many excellent people who were "outsiders."

This is true of some whom we meet on the pages of the Bible as well as in our daily living. I do not know the name of that ardent soul whom John found engaged in casting out demons. But I do know that though this man was fighting evil and fighting it victoriously, when John found that he was not of his company he made him quit. This must have given the demons a field day. This was the case because our unknown servant was prevented from doing the job, while John was too busy preventing him to attend to it himself. Thus they both quit. But when John hurried to report the great news to Jesus, he received no commendation. Listen to our Lord: "Do not forbid him. . . . He that is not against us is for us."

> He drew a circle and shut me out,
> A heretic, rebel, a thing to flout.
> But love and I had a way to win,
> We drew a circle and took him in.[1]

I do not know the name of that soldier who witnessed, with a tender heart, the crucifixion of our Lord. He was possibly one of the quartet sent to perform the bloody task. But be that as it may, when the suffering of Jesus reached its terrible climax and there was wrung from him that awful cry, "Eli, Eli, lama sabachthani?" this soldier

[1] Edwin Markham, "Outwitted." Reprinted by permission of Virgil Markham.

had to go into action. The scribes and the Pharisees might scoff. Others might speculate: "It sounds as if he is calling Elijah. Let's wait and see if Elijah will come take him down."

But this soldier, though he did not understand what the Master was saying, though he did not even know who Elijah was, did understand that the dying man was suffering the very tortures of hell. He knew also that one of his sharpest agonies was that of thirst. Therefore, he hurried to dip a sponge into his ration of sour wine, put it on a reed, and hold it to the lips of Jesus. That gift Jesus gladly accepted. How striking that the last act of human kindness shown to our Lord came at the hands of an ignorant pagan. God girded him, though he did not know him.

When I was pastor in Memphis I cannot say how many times I have stopped in one of the cemeteries to look with appreciation upon the statue of a woman. This woman had not been Miss America, nor had she been the chosen mother of the year. She was a one-time prostitute. She had run a house of ill repute. But when yellow fever broke out she gave herself to the nursing of the girls in her charge till they either got well or died. Then she opened her home to the friendless, the frightened, the desperately ill. Day and night she gave herself unstintingly to the task of nursing these till the disease laid its deadly hand upon her. I cannot recall the epitaph that her grateful city carved upon her monument. But here is one that would fit: "I girded you, though you did not know me."

III

While there is a song in this text, there is also a sob. While there is a touch of laughter, there is a shower of tears. This man Cyrus received magnificent gifts. With what amazing intimacy, even tenderness, did God speak to him: "I have called you by name. I have opened doors before you. I have discovered for you hidden treasures. I will go before you and level the mountains." Thus Cyrus had greatly received and had been helped beyond his wildest dreams. But there was one something that he still lacked. While he had received tremendous gifts, he had missed knowing the Giver.

How often that is in part the case even with us who are professing Christians. It is generally far easier for most of us to believe that we have been divinely girded than that we are being so girded even now. How often we have gone about our task with some degree of success, not at the time conscious of God's undergirding, but trusting largely in ourselves, to realize later that our victory was due alone to the girding of God. It is possible to get so absorbed in doing holy things that we lose sight of our holy Lord. Blessed is he who can constantly use his gifts with the realization that the eternal God is his refuge and underneath are the everlasting arms. Such can rejoice not only in his gifts but far more in the Giver. There is no substitute for the Giver.

Perhaps some of you have what we used to call keepsakes. These may be treasures, they may be trifles, but regardless of their intrinsic worth they are to you very dear. Here, for instance, is one—just a rose pressed away in a book. That rose is being kept not for its beauty but because of the memories it brings. As she who prizes it looks at it, she remembers the man who gave it to her in youth's bright morning long ago. Because it reminds her of him, she would not trade it for all the roses that bloom. Yet that rose, as priceless as it is, is no substitute for the one that walked by her side in life's radiant springtime. She has the gift, but the giver is no longer hers.

I have often thought of that wonderful walk taken by Cleopas and his wife on the first Easter morning. They were going home from a new-made grave. That is a familiar road, packed by the feet of millions. But this grave was unique. The one who now lay, as they believed, behind a great stone in Joseph's garden was yesterday the object of their dearest hopes. Therefore their sorrow was too bitter for tears.

Suddenly a winsome stranger joined them and asked them about their troubles. At once they began to tell him about their wonderful prophet, of the great dreams he had stirred in their hearts. Then, as this stranger opened to them the Scriptures, their hearts burned and their leaden feet became jet planes. Too soon they found themselves at the door of their humble little home. As this companion made as if he were going to continue his journey, they lay all but violent hands on him and constrained him saying, "Stay with us." They could not break off a conversation that was so fascinating. Thus invited, he gladly accepted. Then when supper was announced he became both guest and host. He took the loaf, and when he had asked the blessing he broke it and gave it to them. There was something in the way he did it that made them sure. So we read this striking sentence "Their eyes were opened and they recognized him." This was the climax of their experience. Up to this time they had known the girding of a stranger. Now they knew the stranger himself.

A friend of mine told me that while he was speaking to a company of soldiers in a foreign country there was one big, rather uncouth, chap whose heart God touched. When my friend later sought to explain to him the way of life he seemed only perplexed. Then the preacher said, "Try praying." The big fellow answered, "I don't know how to pray." Then, it would seem, without realizing what he was doing, he broke out with a kind of desperation: "Lord, you know I don't know nothing about praying. I never have prayed. But I'll tell you this, if you have any place anywhere that you would like to have a man to die for you, I'd be glad to be that man." Having thus received the gift of longing, he soon came to know the Giver.

"I gird you," says God. That is a great privilege that comes to all of us—high and low, rich and poor, believer and pagan. The fact that you have been kept across the years; the fact that you are here at this moment is due solely to the girding of God. That which branded the brow of the rich farmer with the ugly name, fool, was the fact that he became so absorbed in the gifts that he forgot the Giver. We may take the opposite course. It is our highest wisdom to enable God to say, "I gird you and you know me."